WELCOME HOME

D1636411

Welcome Home

SCRIPTURE, PRAYERS, AND BLESSINGS FOR THE HOUSEHOLD

YEAR OF MATTHEW

Augsburg Fortress
Minneapolis

WELCOME HOME
Scripture, Prayers, and Blessings for the Household, Year of Matthew

Copyright © 1995 Augsburg Fortress. All rights reserved. Except for brief quotations in critical articles or reviews, no part of this book may be reproduced in any manner without prior written permission from the publisher or from the other copyright holders. Write to: Permissions, Augsburg Fortress, 426 S. Fifth St., Box 1209, Minneapolis, MN 55440-1209.

Scripture quotations, unless otherwise noted, are from the New Revised Standard Version Bible © 1989 Division of Christian Education of the National Council of the Churches of Christ in the United States of America. Used by permission.

Revised Common Lectionary copyright © 1992 Consultation on Common Texts (CCT), 1275 K Street, NW, Suite 1202, Washington, DC 20005-4097 USA. All rights reserved.

Editor: Samuel Torvend
Cover and interior design: Lecy Design
Contributors: Karen Flotte, Craig Mueller, Gail Ramshaw

Library of Congress Cataloging-in-Publication Data

Welcome home : Scripture, prayers, and blessings for the household.
    p. cm.
   Contents: [1] Year A
   ISBN 0-8066-2806-5 (pbk. : Year A)
    1. Family—Prayer-books and devotions—English.   2. Church year
meditations.   I. Augsburg Fortress (Publisher)
BV255.W455 1995
242'.2—dc20
                                                            94-45263
                                                                      CIP

The paper used in this publication meets the minimum requirements of American National Standard for Information Sciences—Permanence of Paper for Printed Library Materials, ANSI Z329.48-1984. ∞™

Manufactured in the U.S.A.   10-28065

00   99   98   97   96   95   1   2   3   4   5   6   7   8

TABLE OF CONTENTS

INTRODUCTION

What this book offers

Let us cherish simple forms of prayer: a whispered plea for
help, repetition of a brief phrase of scripture, or the quiet
invocation of God's names. Simple forms of prayer fill the
pages of the Bible. They occur throughout the Sunday worship
of most Christian churches. They are helpful when we have
little time for sustained prayer or reading. Indeed, for many
people the demands of work, school, and household life can
make it difficult or impossible to pray or meditate at a regular
time each day. In such circumstances, *Welcome Home* offers
brief biblical invocations—adapted from the Sunday readings
and liturgy—for prayer throughout the day. They are listed
with the daily readings.

In addition to brief prayers, many Christians mark the movement of the day by praying the **Lord's Prayer** in the morning,
at midday, and in the evening or at bedtime. This prayer,
always prayed at the holy supper, links us to the worship of
the baptized faithful on Sunday: We pray with Christ to *our*
Father and are united to all other Christians through the silent
working of the Holy Spirit.

When it is possible to keep a more regular rhythm of daily
or weekly prayer—either alone or with others—*Welcome
Home* offers a simple pattern for the morning and the evening:
song, psalm, scripture, canticle, prayer. One may use any or

all parts of this daily pattern. During the seasons of the year, this basic pattern is filled with new songs, psalms, and canticles. In addition, prayers, songs, and blessings are offered for waking in the morning and going to bed at night.

For many Christians, daily or Sunday **reading of scripture** is an important practice. In *Welcome Home* the Sunday readings are listed, followed by a reading for each day that parallels the Sunday readings.

While the day may be filled with much busyness, many Christians find it increasingly important to gather for the evening meal as well as for festive meals on special occasions. Whether one eats alone or with others, *Welcome Home* offers a **table prayer** for each season of the year.

Faith is nurtured throughout the daily and seasonal rhythm of life. While we can pray or read scripture on a daily basis, many Christians find it important to mark the changing seasons of the year with customs—old and new—inspired by various cultures throughout the world. Some of these customs are outlined in *Welcome Home* as **blessings for the household**. They can be adapted for any setting. A single portion or the full festive pattern may be celebrated. A larger selection of customs is available in *Welcome the Light: Celebrating Advent/ Christmas/Epiphany in the Home; Come to the Feast: Celebrating Lent/Holy Week/Easter in the Home*; and *Proclaim the Word: Celebrating Summer/Autumn/November in the Home*, all available from Augsburg Fortress, Publishers.

Christians of one particular tradition or communion do not pray in isolation from other Christians. The ecumenical convergence among North Americans reflects a greater sharing among Christians throughout the world. *Welcome Home* reflects this growing ecumenical agreement in the essentials of

Christian prayer while offering songs, prayers, and blessings from a variety of traditions and cultures.

How to use this book

While *Welcome Home* offers patterns of praying alone or with others, it does not legislate one particular pattern. If you have time only to say **a brief prayer during the day**, use the scriptural invocations found in Daily Readings and Prayers, pray the Lord's Prayer, or recite the Gloria Patri. If a household gathers for **one meal in the home**, use the table prayer. When friends or family gather for **a festive occasion** such as Christmas or Easter, use the blessing for that time of the year or the table prayer for the season.

If you live alone, you may usually pray or read scripture by yourself at home. But there are times when friends or family may be invited for a special occasion or holiday. At those times, a particular pattern of prayer in *Welcome Home* may frame the time together: A song may be sung, a brief text of scripture may be read, or a table prayer may be said before a meal. For instance, if friends are invited to decorate a Christmas tree, the blessing for a Christmas tree may be used.

When two or more people gather for a meal, to celebrate a particular holiday, or to welcome the Lord's Day, the prayer may be shared among them with one person leading the invitation and the blessing, others reading scripture or helping with the singing. In households **where children live**, their participation is encouraged where they are capable—whether that is lighting or holding a candle, singing, or reading scripture. *Welcome Home* invites parents to end the day in prayer with their children: read together, say a prayer together, sing a bedtime song together, bless the children before sleep descends.

While certain songs and prayers are selected in this book, each household may know other songs and prayers that possess a great deal of meaning. Use whatever helps you sing and pray!

Welcome Home offers sections for **daily prayer, Sunday,** and **the seasons of the year.**

THE ELEMENTS OF CHRISTIAN PRAYER

Time

The first Christians, being Jews, followed the patterns of prayer present in their religion and culture. They filled the patterns, however, with the life of Jesus Christ. Thus, since the earliest days, Christians have prayed **in the morning, at midday, in the evening, and at bedtime.** The images of the day—sunrise, noon, sunset, nighttime—became ways to understand the presence of Christ throughout the day. And so Christians speak and sing of Christ the light who never sets, Christ the dawning light of God's mercy.

In the middle of the night, Christ rose from the dead and appeared to his followers on Sunday, the first day of the week. He opened the Scriptures to them, he offered them his peace, he broke bread and shared a cup with them, he sent them forth into the world to proclaim the good news in word and deed. For Christians, **Sunday is the day of Christ's resurrection,** when the people of God gather to hear Christ speak in the scripture readings, to celebrate baptism, to receive his peace, and to share his bread and cup with each other.

The center of the Christian year is the **Three Days of Maundy/ Holy Thursday, Good Friday, and Holy Saturday/Easter Sunday,** during which believers celebrate Christ's passover from suffering and death to risen life. The Easter Vigil/Easter Sunday is the primary baptismal festival of the year. The **Forty Days of Lent** invite Christians to examine their faithfulness to God's promises in baptism, to turn away from sin and receive God's mercy. In the **Fifty Days of Easter,** Christians joyously celebrate the presence of the risen Christ and ask what it means to be his followers in public life.

Because Christ—crucified and risen—is the center of our faith, the Christmas season draws our attention to the ever-present Christ who is our Word and our light. During **Advent** we prepare to welcome the Light. We listen to the prophets who announce God's reign of justice and peace. During the **Twelve Days of Christmas** we celebrate the presence of the Word made flesh who is Emmanuel, God with us. The festival of the **Epiphany** marks Christ's manifestation to the nations of the earth and invites Christians to participate in the church's global outreach. The Baptism of the Lord marks the beginning of Jesus' public ministry.

The many **Sundays after Pentecost** correspond to **Summer** and the first two months of **Autumn.** From the feast of All Saints to Christ the King/Reign of Christ, the Sunday readings during **November** draw us to contemplation of the last things: the communion of saints, the resurrection of the body, and life everlasting.

These many feasts and seasons influence the daily and weekly practice of prayer. They present a rhythm that shapes the Christian awareness of God's presence in all seasons of the year and all seasons of human life. They invite us to celebrate this merciful presence in the many customs of the household.

Place

Prayer and reading may take place anywhere in the home: in a bedroom, out in the garden or yard, around the table, in the living room. For many people, it is important to have some visual focus for prayer: a cross or crucifix, a burning candle, a sacred image or icon. Throughout the seasons of the year, the place of prayer can vary: around the Advent wreath, close to the Christmas tree, next to a nativity scene, near a cross, around a bowl of water or vase of flowers, in the light of a burning candle.

Other places may witness our prayer. When visiting the sick or homebound, bring *Welcome Home* with you. When traveling or on vacation, pack *Welcome Home* in your bag. If you are going to a hospital or nursing home, take *Welcome Home* with you. For a visit to a cemetery, use the words of *Welcome Home*.

Words and gestures

We learn the words of faith and their meanings by speaking them, listening to them, praying them, singing them. We also learn the words of faith by letting them speak in **silence:** The reading of scripture invites us to be quiet so that we might truly hear the Word speaking within us.

The faithful people of God pray for the needs of the Christian community, the nation and the world, the sick and dying, and the poor and the needy. We bring the needs of the day or the particular time before God. It is that time when we can speak the truth, trusting in God's mercy. In prayers of intercession, some people fold their **hands** while others open them, palms up.

When we were baptized, the **sign of the cross** was traced on our foreheads. In some Christian communions, the cross is traced on the lips and the heart as well. Since the earliest centuries, Christians have traced the cross on their foreheads or their bodies when they rise in the morning, at prayer, and when they go to bed at night. It is with this simple gesture that women, men, and children are marked for life at baptism.

Parents may bless their children just as friends may bless each other by placing their two **hands on the head** of the other person. It is an intimate gesture as old as Abraham and as new as the mother who places her hands on the head of her young child. Such a gesture conveys favor, affection, and love.

Some people **kneel** as they pray, others **stand** or **sit**. Some people pray while walking, running, or working. The simple gestures of everyday life—open arms in welcome, an embrace, a handshake, washing, planting, eating—can be the gestures of prayer. The more momentous transitions of life—birth, leaving home, entering school, moving and separation, marriage, sickness, birthdays and reunions, dying and death—can be the opportunities for household prayer. May *Welcome Home* assist you in the daily, Sunday, and seasonal rhythm of prayer in the household.

SCRIPTURE

Daily reading of scripture

Many Christians treasure the practice of daily Bible reading. In past centuries family Bible reading was commonplace, and in the United States during the nineteenth century, the Bible was read daily in the public schools. Perhaps this habit is more important for us now than in the past, for we can no longer assume that a majority of our neighbors and friends know the Bible and honor it. We cannot absorb the Bible by osmosis from the culture around us. The baptized need to attend to the tasks of reading the Bible, encountering God's mercy in its pages, discussing its meaning for our time, comparing it with sacred books of other traditions. Daily Bible reading is one way to keep ourselves connected to the Scriptures and to reimmerse ourselves in the mercy of God that they proclaim.

Most people discover that simply plowing straight through the Bible, end to end, is not the most helpful way to read the Scriptures. Even St. Augustine talks about the Bible as "of mountainous difficulty and enveloped in mysteries." Some readers get halfway through Leviticus and, rightly asking what in the world this has to do with them, abandon their endeavor. Despite the fact that we talk about "the Bible" as one book, it is really a collection of about seventy books, written in different times by different writers. Even some individual books were compiled from material of different dates and situations. It is not surprising that people need some kind of plan for reading through this library. Many patterns for daily Bible reading are available, and each has something to commend it.

This daily lectionary

This daily plan is based on the Sunday readings. The idea here is that for worshiping Christians the days of each week flow out from Sunday, the first day of the week and the day of Christ's resurrection. Whether we were present or not, the assembly of believers met for Christian worship and read the appointed readings. The community gathered around Christ as made known in the Scriptures. On most Sundays, the liturgy presents us with a small quilt about Christ: a Gospel reading is the center star, and around it are stitched two other readings, a psalm, several hymns, a sermon, prayers, even an offertory verse or a proper preface or choir anthem. In this daily lectionary, six more readings encircle the Sunday piece.

Many contemporary Christians, including Lutherans, Roman Catholics, Episcopalians, and an increasing number of other Protestants, are using variant forms of the same three-year Sunday lectionary. According to this list of readings, each week's selections from the Bible proclaim the death and resurrection of Christ. As Martin Luther would say, all the Scriptures "show forth Christ." That is, throughout the entire Bible are stories and poems that proclaim God's mercy. According to this daily lectionary, we use our daily Bible reading to expound further on the Sunday readings, to read background to the Gospel's references and images, to read other Old Testament stories that record God's good news, to see what the epistles add to the mix. This lectionary also presupposes that there are some key stories and central passages of the Scriptures that every Christian should review each year. Some of these famous stories never occur in the Sunday lectionary, and it is good to encounter them each year during a week in which they enhance the Gospel reading.

The Gospel

The three-year Sunday lectionary is constructed around the four Gospels. The Gospel of John, which records seven "signs" of Jesus with long accompanying discourses, is read mainly at the major festivals of the year and for significant liturgical events, such as the series of Lenten pre-baptismal Sundays in year A. On most of the Sundays of year A, the Gospel of Matthew is read; in year B, Mark; and in year C, Luke.

This daily lectionary provides one other reading from a Gospel each week, usually on Wednesday. That reading is either (1) a part of the year's Gospel that in some way parallels or illumines the Sunday Gospel; (2) a part of the year's Gospel that is not included in the Sunday readings; or (3) a reading from one of the other three Gospels that parallels or illumines the Sunday reading.

The first reading

In the three-year lectionary as used by many Christians, the first reading in some way parallels or illumines the Gospel reading.

In keeping with the guiding principle that the Gospel reading gives each week its focus, this daily lectionary provides three weekly readings from the Old Testament that in some way parallel or illumine the Sunday Gospel. The selections may include (1) a narrative that illustrates the mercy of God as proclaimed in the Gospel reading; (2) a story in some way similar to the Gospel narrative; (3) a selection that is background for and necessary to our understanding the Gospel reading; (4) a poem or prophetic passage using imagery central to the Gospel reading; or (5) an extended narrative connected to the Sunday's first reading. Sometimes the readings of Monday and Tuesday are two parts of a long Old Testament narrative that relates in some way to Sunday's Gospel reading.

The psalm

In the three-year lectionary, the psalm is chosen to correspond to the first reading.

In this daily lectionary, one reading each week, usually Saturday's, is taken from the Psalms. Sometimes Saturday's psalm is the full psalm of which only a part was appointed for Sunday. Sometimes it is a psalm with similar themes or images. Occasionally it is a psalm cited in the Sunday Gospel reading.

The second reading

In the three-year lectionary, the second reading, taken from the New Testament letters and the Revelation to John, can be one of two types. During the festival half of the church year, from the beginning of Advent through Trinity Sunday, the second reading parallels or illumines the Gospel reading. During the weeks of the Pentecost season, the second reading goes through individual New Testament books one by one, covering their major parts week by week. This is called semi-continuous selection.

In this daily lectionary, one reading from the non-Gospel half of the New Testament is appointed, usually for Friday. This reading is either (1) a part of the book that is not included in the Sunday semi-continuous readings or (2) a reading from another part of the New Testament that parallels or illumines the Sunday Gospel.

How to use this lectionary

One way to use this daily lectionary is to read each day the suggested selection at meal time or in the early morning or before bed. This can be done either privately or with one's household, with or without prayer and singing. Many Christians use their time commuting to work on public transportation as a time for such daily reading. Of course, any of the six readings could be read any day, or two or three combined for a midweek service. However, if Monday's and Tuesday's readings are a set, the sense of their connection to the Sunday reading should be retained.

Highlighting all the Sunday and festival readings in a Bible would reveal that very little of the Bible is read over the three-year Sunday cycle. Any course of daily Bible reading will acquaint us with more of the Bible than the Sunday readings can, and this particular daily lectionary will do so in such a way as to strengthen our reception of the Sunday readings themselves. Sunday begins not only our week, but our week's reading through the Bible as well. Sunday centers us in the Christian community, and with this plan of daily Bible reading, we remain connected to that Sunday until the next Sunday comes.

THE GOSPEL OF MATTHEW

Each Gospel writer presents a portrait of Jesus slightly different from the other evangelists: Mark begins with the adult Jesus and his public ministy; Matthew and Luke begin with the birth at Bethlehem; John begins with a hymn to the Word. While sharing a common faith in the Lord Jesus, the four evangelists present different images of his life and ministry. Thus, from the perspective of one Gospel, the reader encounters the particular concerns of that author and the community of faith for which the Gospel was written.

Matthew's account presents the life of Jesus from his birth, through the public ministry, to his suffering, death, and resurrection. In this regard Matthew's Gospel may appear to be a biography, but it is much more than that. It is a proclamation of a powerful and living person who speaks to us in the present moment. The questions he asks of the disciples, he asks of us. The invitations and blessings he offers to his first followers, he extends to his contemporary disciples.

In contrast to the other Gospels, Matthew's witness to the crucified and risen Lord has a strong Jewish flavor. The evangelist may have lived in Syria or some other area in which Jewish influence was strong. Scripture scholars suggest that Matthew's Christian community was a mix of Jewish and Gentile believers, those who knew the Scriptures and worship practices of Israel and those who were unfamiliar with them. In this Gospel it is not difficult to discover the Jewishness of Jesus as well as his compassionate outreach to the Gentiles. Numerous quotations from the Old Testament are associated with the person and mission of Jesus. Indeed, Matthew uses images and titles from the Hebrew Scriptures to describe Jesus (Messiah/Anointed One, Emmanuel/God is with us, Shepherd of Israel, Son of David, Wisdom). Many of these images were the inspiration for the O-Antiphons that are prayed during the Advent season.

At times Jesus is presented as a teacher or inspired leader, a new Moses. As Israel's ancient leader went up to Mount Sinai and there received the Law from God, so Jesus ascends a mountain and announces God's blessing (the Beatitudes) on the people. It is an intentional comparison to show Jesus' continuity with Jewish tradition and the startling newness of his life and ministry.

Of particular interest is the manner in which Matthew presents Jesus' teaching. Between chapters 1–2 and 26–28, the evangelist presents five speeches or discourses of Jesus: the Sermon on the Mount (5–7); the missionary speech (10), the parables of the reign of God (13), advice to a divided community (18), and the discourse on the last things (24–25). In these speeches

Matthew shows Jesus teaching through his living word. But Jesus not only speaks the depth of God's love for the world, he lives this love through actions: he heals the sick, forgives his enemies, eats with well-known sinners, feeds the hungry, cares for outsiders, searches after the lost ones, accepts suffering and death.

Indeed, it is in his narration of the Passion that Matthew proclaims the unique character of Jesus the Messiah. He is not a political figure, a ruler who cleverly uses power to his own advantage. He does not attack his critics. He does not rule from a throne at the center of a capital city. He is the Messiah who confounds his accusers with silence. He is the Messiah who reigns from the tree of death. He is the Messiah whose only power is suffering love. In silence and suffering, Jesus embodies the mercy of God. This is his most profound "teaching."

In all this, we come to know that Jesus is more than a good and virtuous person who follows the commandments. He is the living way to God. He is the living image of God's love and blessing for all people. In a world tragically divided by the many manifestations of sin, he is the living source of reconciliation, healing, and unity.

At the beginning of Matthew's Gospel, Jesus is named Emmanuel/God is with us (1:23). It is this name that reveals the promise that wherever two or three are gathered in his name, he is with them (18:20). In Christ, God is with the faithful in the word, in the life-giving waters of baptism, in the bread and cup of the holy supper, in the passage of life, in birth and in death. It is not surprising that the last words of the risen Christ echo this gracious promise: "Remember, I am with you always, to the end of the age" (28:20).

DAILY PRAYER

In a society caught up in the demanding rhythm of schedules and the ever-present voice of radio and television, daily prayer is a welcome practice for those who seek to hear God's voice and cultivate an inner life. Whether one prays alone or with others, the rhythm of daily prayer reveals the life-sustaining communion to which God invites all human beings. Such prayer is a serene power silently at work, drawing us into the ancient yet vital sources of faith, hope, and love.

Since the earliest days of Christianity, the followers of Jesus have prayed as he did: in the morning, in the evening, and before going to bed. When possible they have prayed, although briefly, at midday. This rhythm of prayer follows the daily cycle—sunrise, noon, sunset, nighttime—and allows Christians to recognize the living presence of Christ in all times and all places. "If I climb up to heaven, you are there," writes the psalmist, "if I make the grave my bed, you are there also. If I take the wings of morning and dwell in the uttermost parts of the sea, even there your hand will lead me and your right hand hold me fast" (Psalm 139:7-9).

Our prayer may be the simple invocation of Christ's name or the blessing of the Trinity, repeated throughout the day. It may include the reading of a psalm or a selection of scripture. We may pray the Lord's Prayer—the model of all Christian prayer—once or more a day. When members of a household gather for a meal, either the simple or the festive patterns of prayer outlined in *Welcome Home* may be shared among those present.

While Christians gather on the Lord's Day, Sunday, for public worship, much of our time is spent in the home. We first learn the words, the gestures, and the songs of faith in the home. We discover our essential identity as a community of faith in the home. We mark the many significant transitions of life—from birth to death—in the home. To surround and infuse daily life with the words and gestures of Christian prayer is to discover the ancient yet contemporary truth of the gospel: The ordinary and the human can reveal the mystery of God and divine grace.

Like planets around the sun, our daily prayer draws us to the Sunday assembly where we gather for the word and the breaking of the bread in the changing seasons of the year. From the Sunday assembly, our daily prayer flows into the week.

> Christ the path and Christ the door.
> Christ the bread and welcome cup.
> Christ the word and cleansing bath.
> Christ the robe and Christ the fire.
> Christ the dawn and blazing sun.
> Christ the light and Christ the star.
> Christ the beginning and the end.
> Christ our life and Christ our home.

THE LORD'S PRAYER

Jesus was praying in a certain place, and after he had finished, one of his disciples said to him, "Lord, teach us to pray."
Luke 11:1

The Lord's Prayer is the foundation of Christian prayer. Whether it is recited silently by one person or sung by a community gathered to receive communion, its few lines are cherished by Christians throughout the world. When no other prayers can be prayed, Christians may pray the Lord's Prayer—in the morning, during the day, and in the evening.

Our Father in heaven, hallowed be your name,
your kingdom come, your will be done, on earth as in heaven.
Give us today our daily bread.
Forgive us our sins as we forgive those who sin against us.
Save us from the time of trial and deliver us from evil.
For the kingdom, the power, and the glory are yours,
now and forever. Amen.
    Matthew 6:9-13 with doxology

Our Father, who art in heaven, hallowed be thy name,
thy kingdom come, thy will be done, on earth as it is in heaven.
Give us this day our daily bread; and forgive us our trespasses,
as we forgive those who trespass against us;
and lead us not into temptation, but deliver us from evil.
For thine is the kingdom, and the power, and the glory,
forever and ever. Amen.

Father, hallowed be your name.
Your kingdom come.
Give us each day our daily bread.
And forgive us our sins,
for we ourselves forgive everyone indebted to us.
And do not bring us to the time of trial.
    Luke 11:2-4

THE GLORIA PATRI

To the one seated on the throne and to the Lamb
be blessing and honor and glory and might forever and ever!
    Revelation 5:13

Among those most ancient prayers of praise to the Holy Trinity
is the "Gloria Patri," a Latin title that refers to its first words:
Glory to the Father.

These words of praise are derived, in form, from Jewish
prayers at the time of Jesus. They are similar in content to
the end of the Lord's Prayer, Romans 16:27, Philippians 4:20,
and Revelation 5:13. The naming of the Three Persons accords
with the baptismal formula in Matthew 28:19.

By the end of the fourth century, Christians were singing or
reciting this acclamation at the end of psalms. Metrical para-
phrases—found at the end of many hymns—were in use a
few centuries later.

The Gloria Patri may be recited by itself as a prayer throughout the day. It may also be prayed at the end of a psalm.

Glory to the Father,
and to the Son,
and to the Holy Spirit:
as it was in the beginning,
is now,
and will be for ever. Amen.

UPON WAKING

Upon waking, one may make the sign of the cross and say:

In the name of the Father, and of the Son, and of the Holy Spirit. Amen.

or

The Sacred Three be over me,
the blessing of the Trinity.

For every day

O LORD, in the morning you hear my voice;
in the morning I plead my case to you, and watch.
   Psalm 5:3

Sleeper, awake!
   Rise from the dead,
and Christ will shine on you.   *Ephesians 5:14*

I arise today
   through God's strength to pilot me:
   God's might to uphold me,
   God's wisdom to guide me,
   God's eye to look before me,
   God's ear to hear me,
   God's hand to guard me,
   God's way to lie before me,
   God's shield to protect me.
   Saint Patrick's Breastplate

For Sunday

Glory to God in the highest,
and peace to God's people on earth.

Lord God, heavenly King,
almighty God and Father,
    we worship you, we give you thanks,
    we praise you for your glory.

Lord Jesus Christ, only Son of the Father,
Lord God, Lamb of God,
you take away the sin of the world:
    have mercy on us;
you are seated at the right hand of the Father:
    receive our prayer.

For you alone are the Holy One,
you alone are the Lord,
you alone are the Most High,
    Jesus Christ,
    with the Holy Spirit,
    in the glory of God the Father. Amen.
      Gloria in excelsis Deo (Luke 2:14 with acclamations)

Blessing, honor, glory, and might
be to God and the Lamb forever. Amen.   *See Revelation 5:13*

Holy, holy, holy Lord, God of power and might,
heaven and earth are full of your glory.
    Hosanna in the highest.
    Sanctus (Isaiah 6:3, adapted)

Waking prayers

I give thanks to you, my heavenly Father,
through Jesus Christ your dear Son,
that you have protected me through the night
from all harm and danger
and I ask that you would also protect me today
from sin and every danger,
so that my life and actions may please you.
Into your hands I commend my body, my soul,
and all that is mine.

Let your holy angel be with me,
so that the wicked foe may have no power over me.
Amen.
Luther's morning prayer

Jesus, bright morning star,
show us your mercy.
See Revelation 22:16

MORNING PRAYER

One may trace a cross on the lips and say:

O Lord, open my lips,
   and my mouth shall declare your praise.
Glory to the Father, and to the Son, and to the Holy Spirit:
   as it was in the beginning, is now, and will be forever.
Amen.

Hymn to Christ the Light

O Splendor of the Father's light

O Splendor of the Father's light
that makes our daylight lucid, bright;
O Light of light and sun of day,
now shine on us your brightest ray.

True Sun, break out on earth and shine
in radiance with your light divine;
by dazzling of your Spirit's might,
oh, give our jaded senses light.

The Father sends his Son, our Lord,
to be his bright and shining Word;
come, Lord, ride out your gleaming course
and be our dawn, our light's true source.

Text: St. Ambrose; tr. Gracia Grindal
Tune: CANONBURY (Lord, speak to us, that we may speak)

Morning psalm

With gratitude in your hearts sing psalms . . . to God.
Colossians 3:16

Come, let us sing to the LORD;
  let us shout for joy to the Rock of our salvation.

Let us come before God's presence with thanksgiving
  and raise a loud shout to the LORD with psalms.

For the LORD is a great God,
  and a great Sovereign above all gods.

The LORD holds the caverns of the earth,
  and sustains the heights of the hills.

The sea belongs to God, who made it,
  whose hands have molded the dry land.

Come, let us bow down, and bend the knee,
  and kneel before the LORD our Maker.

For the LORD is our God,
  and we are the people of God's pasture and the sheep of
    God's hand.   *Psalm 95:1-7*

Reading

The sun of righteousness shall rise,
with healing in its wings.   Malachi 4:2

From the daily readings or

Blessed be the God and Father of our Lord Jesus Christ! By
his great mercy he has given us a new birth into a living hope
through the resurrection of Jesus Christ from the dead.
  1 Peter 1:3

Silence

The Song of Zechariah

By the tender mercy of our God,
the dawn from on high will break upon us.　　　*Luke 1:78*

Blessed are you, Lord, the God of Israel,
you have come to your people and set them free.
You have raised up for us a mighty Savior,
born of the house of your servant David.
Through your holy prophets, you promised of old
　　to save us from our enemies,
　　from the hands of all who hate us,
　　to show mercy to our forebears,
　　and to remember your holy covenant.
This was the oath you swore to our father Abraham:
　　to set us free from the hands of our enemies,
　　free to worship you without fear,
　　holy and righteous before you,
　　all the days of our life.

And you, child, shall be called the prophet of the Most High,
for you will go before the Lord to prepare the way,
to give God's people knowledge of salvation
by the forgiveness of their sins.
In the tender compassion of our God
the dawn from on high shall break upon us,
to shine on those who dwell in darkness
and the shadow of death,
and to guide our feet into the way of peace.
　　Benedictus (Luke 1:68-79)

Prayers

Satisfy us with your love in the morning
and we will live this day in joy and praise.
    See Psalm 90:14

Prayer for others and ourselves

The Lord's Prayer

O Lord, almighty and everlasting God,
you have brought us in safety to this new day;
preserve us with your mighty power,
that we may not fall into sin, nor be overcome in adversity;
and in all we do, direct us to the fulfilling of your purpose;
through Jesus Christ our Lord. Amen.

Conclusion

May the God of hope fill you with all joy and peace in be-
lieving, so that you may abound in hope by the power of the
Holy Spirit. Amen.
    Romans 15:13

AT NOON

May God be glorified in all things through Jesus Christ.

In daily labor

Those who wait for the LORD shall renew their strength,
    they shall mount up with wings like eagles,
they shall run and not be weary,
    they shall walk and not faint.   *Isaiah 40:31*

In service to others

Whatever you do, in word or deed,
do everything in the name of the Lord Jesus,
giving thanks to God the Father through him.
    Colossians 3:17

In study

Lead me in your truth, and teach me,
    for you are the God of my salvation.   *Psalm 25:5*

Psalm

They will hunger no more, and thirst no more;
    the sun will not strike them, nor any scorching heat.
    Revelation 7:16

I lift up my eyes to the hills;
    from where is my help to come?

My help comes from the LORD,
    the maker of heaven and earth.

The LORD will not let your foot be moved,
and the One who watches over you will not fall asleep.

Behold, the One who keeps watch over Israel
shall neither slumber nor sleep.

It is the LORD who watches over you;
the LORD is your shade at your right hand,

So that the sun shall not strike you by day,
nor the moon by night.

The LORD shall preserve you from all evil;
the LORD shall keep you safe.

The LORD shall watch over your going out and your coming
in,
from this time forth for evermore.   *Psalm 121*

Reading

We know love by this, that he laid down his life for us—and we ought to lay down our lives for one another. How does God's love abide in anyone who has the world's goods and sees a brother or sister in need and yet refuses help?

Little children, let us love, not in word or speech, but in truth and action.   *1 John 3:16-18*

Prayers

Prayers for others and ourselves

The Lord's Prayer

Blessed Savior,
at this hour you hung upon the cross,
stretching out your loving arms:
Grant that all the peoples of the earth
may look to you and be saved;
for your tender mercies' sake. Amen.

Conclusion

May the God of peace be with us.

EVENING PRAYER

As a candle is lighted:

The city has no need of sun or moon to shine on it,
for the glory of God is its light, and its lamp is the Lamb.
Revelation 21:23

Hymn to Christ the Light

Jesus, joyous light of glory,

Jesus, joyous light of glory, holy and blest,
Son of the immortal Father, highest and best:
Now while day to night surrenders,
in the sunset's fading splendor,
songs of praise to you we render—
    Lord, be our rest.

Christ, of all life's good the Giver, with one accord
you are worthy, now and ever, to be adored;
so the world its glory bringing,
joins celestial voices ringing:
Father, Son and Spirit singing—
    "one holy Lord!"
    Text: Greek hymn, 3rd cent.; para. Stephen P. Starke
    Tune: AR HYD Y NOS (God, who made the earth and heaven)

Evening psalm

Let my prayer rise before you as incense;
the lifting of my hands as the evening sacrifice.
Psalm 141:2

I call upon you O LORD; come quickly to me;
    give ear to my voice when I call to you.

Let my prayer be counted as incense before you,
and the lifting up of my hands as an evening sacrifice.

Set a guard over my mouth, O LORD;
keep watch over the door of my lips.
Do not turn my heart to any evil,
to busy myself with wicked deeds
in company with those who work iniquity;
do not let me eat of their delicacies.

Let the righteous strike me;
let the faithful correct me.
Never let the oil of the wicked anoint my head,
for my prayer is continually against their wicked deeds.

But my eyes are turned toward you, O GOD, my Lord;
in you I seek refuge; do not leave me defenseless.
Keep me from the trap that they have laid for me,
and from the snares of evildoers.

Let the wicked fall into their own nets,
while I alone escape.   *Psalm 141:1-5, 8-10*

Reading

Your word is a lamp to my feet and a light to my path.
Psalm 119:105

From the daily readings or

I appeal to you therefore, brothers and sisters, by the mercies
of God, to present your bodies as a living sacrifice, holy and
acceptable to God, which is your spiritual worship. Do not
be conformed to this world, but be transformed by the renewing of your minds, so that you may discern what is the
will of God—what is good and acceptable and perfect.
Romans 12:1-2

Silence

The Song of Mary

You have come to the aid of your servant Israel,
to remember the promise of mercy.   *Luke 1:54*

My soul proclaims the greatness of the Lord,
my spirit rejoices in God my Savior,
   for you, Lord, have looked with favor on your lowly servant.

From this day all generations will call me blessed:
   you, the Almighty, have done great things for me
   and holy is your name.
   You have mercy on those who fear you,
   from generation to generation.

You have shown strength with your arm
and scattered the proud in their conceit,
casting down the mighty from their thrones
and lifting up the lowly.

You have filled the hungry with good things
and sent the rich away empty.

You have come to the aid of your servant Israel,
to remember the promise of mercy,
the promise made to our forebears,
to Abraham and his children for ever.
   Magnificat (Luke 1:46-55)

Prayers

To you, O LORD, I lift up my soul.
O my God, in you I trust.   Psalm 25:1

Prayers for others and ourselves

The Lord's Prayer

Keep watch, dear Lord,
with those who work, or watch, or weep this night,
and give your angels charge over those who sleep.
Tend the sick, Lord Christ;
give rest to the weary, bless the dying, sooth the suffering,
pity the afflicted, shield the joyous;
and all for your love's sake. Amen.

Conclusion

May the Lord, who is our peace,
give us peace at all times and in every way.
  See 2 Thessalonians 3:16

AT BEDTIME

Upon retiring, one may make the sign of the cross and say:

May the all-powerful Lord grant us a restful night
and a peaceful death.

Psalm

They need no light of lamp or sun,
for the Lord God will be their light.   *Revelation 22:5*

Come, bless the LORD, all you servants of the LORD,
    who stand by night in the house of the LORD!
Lift up your hands to the holy place,
    and bless the LORD.

May the LORD, maker of heaven and earth,
    bless you from Zion.   *Psalm 134*

Reading

The Lamb will be their shepherd,
    and he will guide them to springs of the water of life,
and God will wipe away every tear from their eyes.
    Revelation 7:17

Come to me, all you that are weary and are carrying heavy
burdens, and I will give you rest. Take my yoke upon you,
and learn from me; for I am gentle and humble in heart, and
you will find rest for your souls. For my yoke is easy, and
my burden is light.
    Matthew 11:28-30

The Song of Simeon

Guide us waking, O Lord, and guard us sleeping;
that awake we may watch with Christ
and asleep we may rest in peace.

Now, Lord, you let your servant go in peace;
your word has been fulfilled.
My own eyes have seen the salvation
which you have prepared in the sight of every people:
a light to reveal you to the nations
and the glory of your people Israel.
    Nunc dimittis (Luke 2:29-32)

Prayers

Into your hand I commit my spirit;
    you have redeemed me, O LORD, faithful God.
    Psalm 31:5

Prayer for others and ourselves

The Lord's Prayer

I give thanks to you, my heavenly Father,
through Jesus Christ your dear Son,
that you have graciously protected me today,
and I ask you to forgive me all my sins,
where I have done wrong,
and graciously to protect me tonight.
For into your hands I commend myself:
my body, my soul, and all that is mine.
Let your holy angel be with me,
so that the wicked foe may have no power over me.
Amen.
    Luther's evening prayer

or

Visit this house,
we beg you, Lord,
and banish from it
the deadly power of the evil one.
May your holy angels dwell here
to keep us in peace,
and may your blessing be always upon us.
We ask this through Christ our Lord. Amen.

Night prayers with children

Now I lay me down to sleep,
I pray the Lord my soul to keep.
And in the morning light I wake,
I pray the path of love to take.

Now I lay me down to sleep,
I pray the Lord my soul to keep.
God's love stay with me through the night
and keep me safe till morning light.

Lord, keep us safe this night,
    secure from all our fears.
May angels guard us while we sleep,
    till morning light appears.

Keep us, O Lord, as the apple of your eye;
shelter us under the shadow of your wings.

Night blessings for children

A parent may trace the cross on the child's forehead or heart and say one of these blessings:

May God protect you through the night.

May the Lord Jesus keep you in his love.

May the Holy Spirit bless you with peace.

Receive the cross of Christ.

May Christ, the good shepherd, watch over you through the night.

Stay with us, Lord.

May the light of Christ be with us.

Night songs for children

Go, my children, with my blessing

Go, my children, with my blessing, never alone;
waking, sleeping, I am with you, you are my own;
in my love's baptismal river I have made you mine forever,
go, my children, with my blessing, you are my own.
> Text: Jaroslav Vajda
> Tune: AR HYD Y NOS (God, who made the earth and heaven)

All praise to thee, my God

All praise to thee, my God, this night
for all the blessings of the light.
Keep me, oh, keep me, King of kings,
beneath thine own almighty wings.

Oh, may my soul in thee repose,
and may sweet sleep mine eyelids close,
sleep that shall me more vig'rous make
to serve my God when I awake!

Text: Thomas Ken
Tune: TALLIS' CANON

O Christ, you are the light

O Christ, you are the light and day;
you drive the gloom of night away;
grant, Light of light, your Word to show
the light of heav'n to us below.

All holy Lord, in humble prayer
we ask tonight your watchful care
and pray that our repose may be
a quiet night, from perils free.

Text: Latin hymn, 6th cent.; tr. William Copeland
Tune: OLD HUNDREDTH (Praise God from whom all blessings flow) or TALLIS' CANON

Children of the heavenly Father

Children of the heav'nly Father
safely in his bosom gather;
nestling bird or star in heaven
such a refuge ne'er was given.

Though he giveth or he taketh,
God his children ne'er forsaketh;
his the loving purpose solely
to preserve them pure and holy.

> Text: Carolina Sandell Berg; tr. Ernst Olson
> Tune: Swedish folk tune

All through the night

Sleep, my child, and peace attend thee, all through the night;
guardian angels God will send thee, all through the night;
soft the drowsy hours are creeping,
   hill and vale in slumber sleeping,
I my loving vigil keeping, all through the night.

While the moon her watch is keeping, all through the night;
while the weary world is sleeping, all through the night;
o'er thy spirit gently stealing, visions of delight revealing,
breathes a pure and holy feeling, all through the night.

> Text: Traditional
> Tune: AR HYD Y NOS (God, who made the earth and heaven)

FOR READING WITH CHILDREN THROUGHOUT THE YEAR

Advent

Grindal, Gracia. *Good News of Great Joy.* Minneapolis: Augsburg Fortress, 1994.

Christmas

Berger, Barbara. *The Donkey's Dream.* New York: The Putnam Publishing Group, Philomel Books, 1986.

Davis, Inez Torres. *Modestita's Gift: A Christmas Story; El Regalo de Modestita: Una Historia para la Navidad.* Minneapolis: Augsburg, 1991. The story is told in both English and Spanish.

De Brebeuf, Jean. *The Huron Carol.* New York: Dutton Children's Books, 1992.

Langstaff, John. *What a Morning! The Christmas Story in Black Spirituals.* New York: Margaret K. McElderry Books, Macmillan Children's Book Group, 1987.

Rosen, Michael. *Elijah's Angel.* San Diego: Harcourt Brace Jovanovich, 1992. A story of Jewish/Christian relationship.

Wilner, Isabel. *B is for Bethlehem.* New York: Dutton Children's Books, 1990.

Epiphany

De Paola, Tomie. *The Legend of Old Befana.* New York: Harcourt Brace Jovanovich, 1980.

Manson, Christopher. *A Gift for the King.* New York: Henry Holt and Company, 1989.

Wangerin, Walter, Jr. *Branta and the Golden Stone.* New York: Simon and Schuster, 1993.

Lent

O'Neal, Debbie Trafton. *Before and After Easter: Activities and Ideas for Lent to Pentecost.* Minneapolis: Augsburg, 1992.

Holy Week/Easter Vigil

Hunt, Angela Elwell. *The Tale of Three Trees.* Batavia, IL: Lion Publishing Corporation, 1989. (Also for Holy Cross Day)

Hutton, Warwick. *Moses in the Bulrushes.* New York: Margaret K. McElderry Books, Macmillan Children's Book Group, 1986.

Spier, Peter. *Noah's Ark.* New York: Doubleday, 1977; Dell, 1992.

Waskow, Arthur, et al. *Before There Was a Before.* New York: Adama Books, 1984.

Easter

Gibbons, Gail. *Easter.* New York: Holiday House, 1989.

Maxwell, Cassandre. *Yosef's Gift of Many Colors.* Minneapolis: Augsburg, 1993.

Nerlove, Miriam. *Easter.* Niles, IL: Albert Whitman & Co., 1989.

O'Neal, Debbie Trafton. *Before and After Easter: Activities and Ideas for Lent to Pentecost.* Minneapolis: Augsburg, 1992.

Other stories

African American stories:

Climbing Jacob's Ladder: Heroes of the Bible in African-American Spirituals. Ed. John Langstaff. New York: Margaret K. McElderry Books, Macmillan Children's Book Group, 1991.

Hamilton, Virginia. *The People Could Fly: American Black Folktales.* New York: Knopf, Alfred A., Books for Young Readers, 1994.

Creation/environment:

De Paola, Tomie. *Francis: The Poor Man of Assisi.* New York: Holiday House, 1982.

Henry, Edward. *A Song for Creation.* Minneapolis: Augsburg, 1993.

SUNDAY

From the earliest days of our history, Christians have called Sunday "the Lord's Day," the first day of the week when God created light. Ancient Christians called the day of Christ's resurrection "the eighth day," a new day on which God brought life and light out of death and darkness. As scripture attests, Christ appears to his followers on Sunday, the first day of the week. He gathers them through the power of the Spirit. He explains the Scriptures and breaks bread. He offers his gift of peace, and sends his disciples forth into the world to continue his mission. For Christians Sunday remains the day on which we celebrate our immersion in his life through baptism and our sustenance in that life through the holy supper. Sunday marks the public gathering of Christians and the renewal of their mission in the rhythm of daily life.

Christians may prepare for the Lord's Day with the setting of the sun on Saturday evening and pray at its end with nightfall on Sunday. In various ways we mark this day: with prayer, song, reading from the Scriptures, renewing our baptism, and joining other Christians for worship. We may celebrate the day of resurrection with a simple invocation of Christ's name or a festive meal surrounded with lights, prayers, and songs. While we gather with the baptized on the Lord's Day for the celebration of word and meal, we recognize that the risen Christ also appears in the many ordinary places of life: in houses and apartments, in a garden and by a lake, in the sharing of a meal, and walking with friends on a road (Luke 24; John 20-21). Celebrating Sunday in the home brings to greater awareness the presence of Christ among us and with us in our daily tasks and gatherings.

The celebration of Sunday may begin simply with the lighting of a candle and a prayer to Christ the Light at the Saturday evening meal or at bedtime. On festive occasions, one may use more lights, a bowl of water, and a greater selection of songs, psalms, and readings. On Sunday morning, one may offer a brief prayer or read a psalm. As the day comes to a close, one may light a candle and pray or sing to Christ the Light, read a selection from the Bible, or simply repeat a short verse of scripture.

SATURDAY EVENING

One may use any or all sections of this vigil prayer.
A candle or lamp and a bowl of water may be used.

As the candle or lamp is lighted:

Jesus Christ is the light of the world:
the light no darkness can overcome.

Hymn to Christ the Light

O radiant Light

O radiant Light, O Sun divine,
of God the Father's deathless face,
O Image of the light sublime
that fills the heavenly dwelling place.

Lord Jesus Christ, as daylight fades,
as shine the lights of eventide,
we praise the Father with the Son,
the Spirit blest and with them one.

O Son of God, the source of life,
praise is your due by night and day;
our [happy] lips must raise the strain
of your proclaimed and splendid name.

> *Text: Greek, 3rd cent.; tr. William G. Storey*
> *Tune: TALLIS' CANON or OLD HUNDREDTH*

Thanksgiving for the Light

We praise and thank you, O God,
through your Son, Jesus Christ our Lord.
Through him you have enlightened us
by revealing the light that never fades.
By dying he has destroyed the power of death.
By rising he has restored life to the whole world.
May his bright light transform the hearts of all believers
and enlighten this world that longs to see him.
We praise and glorify you, O God,
Father, Son, and Holy Spirit,
now and forever.
Amen.

Psalm

*Christ has been raised from the dead,
the first fruits of those who have died.*   *1 Corinthians 15:20*

Give thanks to the LORD, who is good,
   whose mercy endures for ever.

Let Israel now proclaim,
   "The mercy of the LORD endures for ever."

Let the house of Aaron now proclaim,
   "The mercy of the LORD endures forever."

Let those who fear the LORD now proclaim,
   "The mercy of the LORD endures for ever."

The LORD is my strength and my song
   and has become my salvation.

There is a sound of exultation and victory
   in the tents of the righteous:

"The right hand of the LORD has triumphed!

the right hand of the LORD is exalted!
the right hand of the LORD has triumphed!"

I shall not die, but live,
and declare the works of the LORD.
Psalm 118:1-4, 14-17

The Resurrection Gospel

One of the following accounts of the resurrection may be read:

Matthew 28:1-10, 16-20
John 20:1-10

Silence for reflection follows.
When two or more persons have gathered, a brief discussion
of the Gospel may follow.

Thanksgiving for baptism

If used, this thanksgiving may take place around a bowl of
water. If two or more persons are present, one may lead the
opening dialogue and the prayer.

The Lord be with you.
And also with you.
Let us give thanks to the Lord our God.
It is right to give our thanks and praise.

Holy God and mighty Lord, we give you thanks
for you nourish and sustain us and all living things
with the gift of water.
In the beginning your Spirit moved over the waters
and you created heaven and earth.
By the waters of the flood you saved Noah and his family.
You led Israel through the sea out of slavery

and into the promised land.
In the waters of the Jordan
your Son was baptized by John and anointed with the Spirit.
By the baptism of his death and resurrection
your Son set us free from sin and death
and opened the way to everlasting life.

We give you thanks, O God,
that you have given us new life in the water of baptism.
Buried with Christ in his death,
you raise us to share in his resurrection
by the power of the Holy Spirit.
May all who have passed through the water of baptism
continue in the risen life of our Savior.
To you be all honor and glory, now and forever.
Amen.

*Each person may dip a hand into the water and make the
sign of the cross in remembrance of his or her baptism.*

Prayer

Prayers for others and ourselves

The Lord's Prayer

O God,
in the darkness of night
you raised your Son from the dead.
Raise us to new life in him
and strengthen us to serve you.
May your words be on our lips,
your love in our hearts,
and your strength in our work.
We ask this through Christ our Lord.
Amen.

Blessing

The almighty God,
the Father, the Son, and the Holy Spirit,
bless us with peace.
Amen. [Alleluia.]

SUNDAY MORNING

One may use any or all portions of this section.

Blessed be the God and Father of our Lord Jesus Christ! By his great mercy he has given us a new birth into a living hope through the resurrection of Jesus Christ from the dead.
1 Peter 1:3

This is the feast of victory for our God.
Alleluia, alleluia, alleluia.

Christ has died. Christ is risen. Christ will come again.

Psalm

This is the day that the LORD has made;
let us rejoice and be glad in it.   *Psalm 118:24*

The stone that the builders rejected
  has become the chief cornerstone.
This is the LORD's doing;
  it is marvelous in our eyes.

This is the day that the LORD has made;
  let us rejoice and be glad in it.
Save us, we beseech you, O LORD!
  O LORD, we beseech you, give us success!

Blessed is the one who comes in the name of the LORD.
  We bless you from the house of the LORD.
The LORD is God, and he has given us light.
  Bind the festal procession with branches,
    up to the horns of the altar.

You are my God, and I will give thanks to you;
  you are my God, I will extol you.

O give thanks to the LORD, for he is good,
  for his steadfast love endures forever.
    Psalm 118:22-29

Reading

As many of you as were baptized into Christ
have clothed yourselves with Christ.   *Galatians 3:27*

On the first day of the week, at early dawn, *the women* came
to the tomb, taking the spices that they had prepared. They
found the stone rolled away from the tomb, but when they
went in, they did not find the body. While they were perplexed
about this, suddenly two men in dazzling clothes stood beside
them. The women were terrified and bowed their faces to
the ground, but the men said to them, "Why do you look for
the living among the dead? He is not here, but has risen.
Remember how he told you, while he was still in Galilee,
that the Son of Man must be handed over to sinners, and be
crucified, and on the third day rise again."   *Luke 24:1-7*

Canticle of praise

God raised Jesus up, having freed him from death,
because it was impossible for him to be held in its power.
    Acts 2:24

We praise you, O God,
we acclaim you as Lord;
all creation worships you,
the Father everlasting.
To you all angels, all the powers of heaven,
the cherubim and seraphim, sing in endless praise:
    Holy, holy, holy Lord, God of power and might,
    heaven and earth are full of your glory.
The glorious company of apostles praise you.

The noble fellowship of prophets praise you.
The white-robed army of martyrs praise you.
Throughout the world the holy Church acclaims you:
   Father, of majesty unbounded,
    your true and only Son, worthy of all praise,
    the Holy Spirit, advocate and guide.

You, Christ, are the king of glory,
the eternal Son of the Father.
When you took our flesh to set us free
you humbly chose the Virgin's womb.
You overcame the sting of death
and opened the kingdom of heaven to all believers.
You are seated at God's right hand in glory.
We believe that you will come to be our judge.
   Come then, Lord, and help your people,
    bought with the price of your own blood,
    and bring us with your saints
    to glory everlasting.
    Te Deum laudamus

Prayers

For others and ourselves

The Lord's Prayer

O God,
for our redemption
you gave your only Son to suffer death on the cross,
and by his glorious resurrection
you delivered us from the power of death.

Make us die every day to sin,
so that we may rise to live with Christ forever;
who lives and reigns with you and the Holy Spirit, one God,
now and forever.
Amen.

Preparing to join the worshiping assembly

O send out your light and your truth;
   let them lead me;
let them bring me to your holy hill
   and to your dwelling.
Then I will go to the altar of God,
   to God my exceeding joy.   *Psalm 43:3-4*

I was glad when they said to me,
   "Let us go to the house of the LORD!"   *Psalm 122:1*

Preparing to hear the word

You word is a lamp to my feet
   and a light to my path.   *Psalm 119:105*

Lord, to whom can we go?
You have the words of eternal life.   *John 6:68*

May the gospel be in our minds,
on our lips, and in our hearts.

Preparing to receive the bread and cup

Taste and see that the LORD is good;
   happy are they who trust in the LORD!   *Psalm 34:8*

Lord, give us the bread that never fails.   *See John 6:34*

May we receive our Lord with a living faith
as he comes to us in his holy supper.

Praying before a Sunday meal

The creatures of the earth look to you
   to give them their food in due season;
when you give to them, they gather it up;
    when you open your hand, they are filled with good things.
    Psalm 104:27-28

Blessed are you, O Lord our God,
who give nourishment to all your creatures.
Fill our hearts with joy and gladness
so that, strengthened by this meal,
we may abound in all good works,
in Christ Jesus, our Lord.
Blessed are you, O Lord our God,
who fill the world with light and life.
    adapted from the Apostolic Constitutions

We thank you, our Father,
for the life and knowledge
which you have revealed to us through Jesus your Child.
   Glory be yours through all ages!
Just as the bread broken
was first scattered on the hills,
then was gathered and became one,
so let your Church be gathered
from the ends of the earth into your kingdom,
for yours is glory and power through all ages.
    from the Didache

SUNDAY EVENING

One may use any or all sections of this prayer.
A candle or a lamp may be used.

As the candle or lamp is lighted:

Stay with us, Lord, because it is almost evening
and the day is now nearly over.   *See Luke 24:29*

Evening hymn

O Christ, you are the light

O Christ, you are the light and day
   which drives away the night,
the ever shining Sun of God
   and pledge of future light.

As now the evening shadows fall
   oh, grant us, Lord, we pray,
a quiet night to rest in you
   until the break of day.

Regard, O Lord, our helplessness
   and come to our defense;
may we be governed by your love,
   in true obedience.

Remember us, poor mortals all,
   we humbly ask, O Lord,
and may your presence in our souls
   be now our great reward.
    Text: Christe qui Lux es et Dies, c. 800; tr. Frank C. Quinn, O.P.
    Tune: ST. ANNE (O God, our help in ages past)
    or LAND OF REST (Jerusalem, my happy home)

Psalm

This Jesus God raised up,
. . . being exalted at the right hand of God.   Acts 2:32-33

The LORD said to my lord, "Sit at my right hand,
    until I make your enemies your footstool."

The LORD will send the scepter of your power out of Zion,
    saying, "Rule over your enemies round about you.

Nobility has been yours from the day of your birth;
    in the beauty of holiness have I begotten you,
    like dew from the womb of the morning."

The LORD has sworn and will not recant:
    "You are a priest for ever after the order of Melchizedek."

The lord who is at God's right hand
will smite rulers in the day of his wrath;
    he will rule over the nations.

He will drink from the brook beside the road
    and therefore will lift his head.   *Psalm 110:1-5, 7*

Reading

Look at my hands and my feet; see that it is I myself.
Touch me and see.   Luke 24:39

Now on that same day *(the first day of the week)* two of them
were going to a village called Emmaus, about seven miles
from Jersualem. While they were talking and discussing, Jesus
himself came near and went with them, but their eyes were
kept from recognizing him. As they came near the village to
which they were going, he walked ahead as if he were going
on. But they urged him strongly, saying, "Stay with us, because
it is almost evening and the day is now nearly over." So he

went in to stay with them. When he was at table with them,
he took bread, blessed and broke it, and gave it to them. Then
their eyes were opened, and they recognized him.
Luke 24:13, 15-16, 28-31a

Canticle of praise

All nations will come and worship before you.
Revelation 15:4

[Alleluia!]
Salvation and glory and power to our God,
    for his judgments are true and just.

Praise our God, all you his servants,
and all who fear him, small and great.

The Lord our God the Almighty reigns.
Let us rejoice and exult and give him the glory,
for the marriage of the Lamb has come,
    and his bride has made herself ready.
[Alleluia!]   *Revelation 19:1-2, 5, 6-7*

Prayers

For others and ourselves

The Lord's Prayer

Lord God,
whose Son our Savior Jesus Christ
triumphed over the powers of death
and prepared for us our place in the new Jerusalem:
Grant that we,
who have this day given thanks for the resurrection,
may praise you in that City of which he is the light,
and where he lives and reigns with you and the Holy Spirit,
one God, now and forever.
Amen.

Conclusion

May the grace of the Lord Jesus Christ be with us all.

ADVENT • CHRISTMAS • EPIPHANY

As winter comes to the northern hemisphere, the days grow shorter and the nights grow long. This time of the year speaks of cooler, if not freezing, temperatures, of barren trees, and little growth in gardens and fields. In many parts of North America, the cooler months of winter seem to hold the land in a dark, lifeless grasp.

The words of the psalms and prophets speak of winter as an image of life without God's life, God's light, God's fire. And yet Isaiah makes this marvelous declaration: Upon those who live in a land of deep darkness, the light has shined.

During the winter days of Advent, Christians prepare to welcome the light of God's grace present in human life. Often times, though, the season is perceived as a preparation for the celebration of Jesus' birth, as if the Christian community could somehow return to Bethlehem of old. And yet, the church knows that Christ has already been born, has died, and is risen.

In the days of Advent, Christians prepare to celebrate the presence of God's Word among us in our own day. During these four weeks, we pray that the reign of God, which Jesus preached and lived, would come among us. We pray that God's justice would flourish in our land, that the people of the earth would live in peace, that the weak and the sick and the hungry would be strengthened, healed, and fed with God's merciful presence. During the last days of Advent, Christians welcome Christ with names inspired by the prophets: wisdom, liberator of slaves, mighty power, radiant dawn and sun of justice, the keystone of the arch of humanity, and Emmanuel—God with us.

Over the centuries, various customs have developed which focus the household on welcoming the light of Christ: the daily or weekly lighting of the Advent wreath, the blessing of the lighted Christmas tree, the candle-lit procession of Las Posadas, the flickering lights of the luminaria, the Christ candle at Christmas.

The Christian household not only welcomes the light of Christ at Christmas, but celebrates the presence of that light throughout the Twelve Days, from Christmas until the Epiphany, January 6. These are days of merriment, singing carols, exchanging gifts, visiting the sick and homebound, inviting guests into the home.

On the Epiphany, the household joins the church throughout the world in celebrating the manifestation, the "epiphany," of Christ to the world. The festival of Christmas is thus set within the context of outreach to the larger community; it possesses an outward movement. The festival of the Epiphany asks the Christian household: How might our faith in Christ the Light be shared with friends and family, with our neighbors, with the poor and needy in our land, with those who live in other nations?

In the Christmas season, Christians welcome the light of Christ that is already with us through faith. In word and gesture, prayer and song, in the many customs of diverse cultures, Christians celebrate this life-giving Word and ask that it dwell more deeply in the rhythm of daily life.

ADVENT

The lighting of the Advent wreath may begin daily prayer.
See "Blessing of the Advent wreath."

A hymn for Advent

The King shall come when morning dawns

The King shall come when morning dawns
   and light triumphant breaks,
when beauty gilds the eastern hills
   and life to joy awakes.

Not as of old a little child,
   to bear and fight and die,
but crowned with glory like the sun
   that lights the morning sky.

The King shall come when morning dawns
   and light and beauty brings.
Hail, Christ the Lord! Your people pray:
   Come quickly, King of kings.

    Text: John Brownlie
    Tune: CONSOLATION or ST. ANNE (O God, our help in ages past)

A psalm for Advent

Shower, O heavens, from above,
and let the skies rain down righteousness;
let the earth open, that salvation may spring up.
          Isaiah 45:8

Give ear, O Shepherd of Israel,
    you who lead Joseph like a flock!
You that are enthroned upon the cherubim, shine forth
    before Ephraim and Benjamin and Manasseh.
Stir up your might,
    and come to save us!
Restore us, O God;
    let your face shine, that we may be saved.

O LORD God of hosts,
    how long will you be angry with your people's prayers?
You have fed them with the bread of tears,
    and given them tears to drink in full measure.
You make us the scorn of our neighbors;
    our enemies laugh among themselves.

Restore us, O God of hosts;
    let your face shine, that we may be saved.   *Psalm 80:1-7*

Readings for Advent

See the daily readings

A canticle for Advent

I am coming to gather all nations and tongues;
and they shall come and shall see my glory.   *Isaiah 66:18*

Morning: The Song of Zechariah
Evening: The Song of Mary
Bedtime: The Song of Simeon

From December 17–23, the O-Antiphons introduce the Song
of Mary

or

A shoot shall come out from the stump of Jesse,
    and a branch shall grow out of his roots.
The spirit of the LORD shall rest on him,
    the spirit of wisdom and understanding,
    the spirit of counsel and might,
    the spirit of knowledge and the fear of the LORD.
His delight shall be in the fear of the LORD.

He shall not judge by what his eyes see,
    or decide by what his ears hear;
but with righteousness he shall judge the poor,
    and decide with equity for the meek of the earth.

The wolf shall live with the lamb,
    the leopard shall lie down with the kid,
the calf and the lion and the fatling together,
    and a little child shall lead them.

They will not hurt or destroy
    on all my holy mountain;
for the earth will be full of the knowledge of the LORD
    as the waters cover the sea.   *Isaiah 11:1-4, 6, 9*

A prayer for Advent

God of all wisdom,
our hearts yearn for the warmth of your love,
and our minds search for the light of your Word.
Increase our longing for Christ our Savior,
and strengthen us to grow in love.
At the dawn of his coming
may we rejoice in his presence
and welcome the light of his truth.
This we ask in the name of Jesus Christ.
Amen.

Advent table prayer

Blessed is he who comes in the name of the Lord.
   Hosanna in the highest!
All the ends of the earth shall see the salvation of our God.
   Amen. Come, Lord Jesus.

Blessed are you, O Lord our God,
the One who is, who was, and who is to come.
At this table you fill us with good things.
May these gifts strengthen us
to share with the hungry and all those in need,
as we wait and watch for your coming among us
in Jesus Christ our Lord.
Amen.

DAILY READINGS AND PRAYERS

First Sunday of Advent

S	Isa. 2:1-5		Ps. 122
	Rom. 13:11-14		Matt. 24:36-44
M	Gen. 6:11-22		
T	Gen. 8:1-19		
W	Matt. 24:23-35		
Th	Gen. 9:8-17		
F	Heb. 11:1-7, 32-40		
S	Ps. 123		

For prayer throughout the day
Let us walk in the light of the LORD.   *Isaiah 2:5*

A prayer for the week
Lord Jesus,
you have said,
"About that day and hour no one knows,
neither the angels of heaven,
nor the Son, but only the Father."
Keep us awake, ready, and prepared
for the day of your coming.
Amen.

Second Sunday of Advent

S	Isa. 11:1-10	Ps. 72:1-7, 18-19
	Rom. 15:4-13	Matt. 3:1-12
M	Isa. 12:1-6	
T	Isa. 40:1-11	
W	John 8:31-36	
Th	Gen. 15:1-6	
F	Acts 13:16-26	
S	Ps. 72	

For prayer throughout the day
Prepare the way of the Lord.   *Matthew 3:3*

A prayer for the week
Faithful God,
grant that we may live in harmony with one another
in Christ our Lord,
so that with one voice we may glorify you.
Amen.

Third Sunday of Advent

S	Isa. 35:1-10	Ps. 146:5-10
	James 5:7-10	Matt. 11:2-11
M	Isa. 29:18-24	
T	Ezek. 47:1-12	
W	John 12:35-50	
Th	Zech. 8:1-17	
F	James 5:11-18	
S	Ps. 146	

For prayer throughout the day

Be strong, do not fear! Here is your God.   *Isaiah 35:4*

A prayer for the week

My soul proclaims the greatness of the Lord,
my spirit rejoices in God my Savior,
for you, Lord, have looked with favor on your lowly servant.
Amen.

Fourth Sunday of Advent

S	Isa. 7:10-16	Ps. 80:1-7, 17-19
	Rom. 1:1-7	Matt. 1:18-25
M	Gen. 17:15-21	
T	Gen. 21:1-21	
W	Matt. 1:1-17	
Th	Gen. 37:2-11	
F	Gal. 3:23—4:7	
S	Ps. 113	

For prayer throughout the day

Emmanuel: God is with us.   *Matthew 1:23*

A prayer for the week

Give ear, O Shepherd of Israel,
you who lead us like a flock.
Restore us, O God;
let your face shine on us, that we may be saved.
Amen.

THE O-ANTIPHONS

December 17

O Wisdom, proceeding from the mouth of the Most High,
pervading and permeating all creation,
mightily ordering all things:
   Come and teach us the way of prudence.

December 18

O Adonai and ruler of the house of Israel,
who appeared to Moses in the burning bush
and gave him the Law on Sinai:
   Come with an outstretched arm and redeem us.

December 19

O Root of Jesse, standing as an ensign before the peoples,
before whom all kings are mute,
to whom the nations will do homage:
   Come quickly to deliver us.

December 20

O Key of David and scepter of the house of Israel,
you open and no one can close,
you close and no one can open:
   **Come and rescue the prisoners who are in darkness
   and the shadow of death.**

December 21

O Dayspring, splendor of light everlasting:
   **Come and enlighten those who sit in darkness
   and in the shadow of death.**

December 22

O King of the nations, the ruler they long for,
the cornerstone uniting all people:
Come and save us all, whom you formed out of clay.

December 23

O Emmanuel, our king and our lawgiver,
the anointed of the nations and their Savior:
Come and save us, O Lord our God.

BLESSING OF THE ADVENT WREATH

*This prayer may be used throughout the Advent season.
If present, a young child may light the candle(s) while an
older child may read the scripture selection or pray the
blessing.*

Invitation

Let us praise Christ who brings us light
now and forever.
Amen.

Reading

As we prepare for the celebration of Christ's coming among
us, let us listen to the words of scripture:

The people who walked in darkness
   have seen a great light;
those who lived in a land of deep darkness—
   on them light has shined.
For a child has been born for us,
   a son given to us;
authority rests upon his shoulders;
   and he is named
Wonderful Counselor, Mighty God,
   Everlasting Father, Prince of Peace.
His authority shall grow continually,
   and there shall be endless peace
for the throne of David and his kingdom.
   He will establish and uphold it with justice and with righ-
      teousness.   *Isaiah 9:2, 6-7a*

Prayer of blessing

Let us pray:

[First Week in Advent]

Blessed are you, O Lord our God, ruler of the universe.
You call all nations to walk in your light
and to seek your ways of justice and peace,
for the night is past, and the dawn of your coming is near.
Bless us as we light the first candle of this wreath.
Rouse us from sleep,
that we may be ready to greet our Lord when he comes
and welcome him into our hearts and homes,
for he is our light and our salvation.
  Blessed be God forever.

The first candle of the Advent wreath is lighted.

[Second Week in Advent]

Blessed are you, O Lord our God, ruler of the universe.
John the Baptist calls all people to prepare the Lord's way
for the kingdom of heaven is near.
Bless us as we light the candles on this wreath.
Baptize us with the fire of your Spirit,
that we may be a light shining in the darkness
welcoming others as Christ has welcomed us,
for he is our light and our salvation.
  Blessed be God forever.

The first two candles of the Advent wreath are lighted.

[Third Week in Advent]

Blessed are you, O Lord our God, ruler of the universe.
Your prophets spoke of a day when the desert would blossom
and waters would break forth in the wilderness.
Bless us as we light the candles on this wreath.
Strengthen our hearts
as we prepare for the coming of the Lord.
May he give water to all who thirst,
for he is our light and our salvation.
Blessed be God forever.

The first three candles of the Advent wreath are lighted.

[Fourth Week in Advent]

Blessed are you, O Lord our God, ruler of the universe.
In your Son, Emmanuel,
you have shown the light of your countenance
and saved us from the power of sin.
Bless us as we light the candles on this wreath.
Increase our longing for your presence,
that at the celebration of your Son's birth
his Spirit might dwell anew in our midst,
for he is our light and our salvation.
Blessed be God forever.

All four candles of the Advent wreath are lighted.

Song

O Savior, rend the heavens wide

Week 1

O Savior, rend the heavens wide;
come down, come down with mighty stride;
unlock the gates, the doors break down;
unbar the way to heaven's crown.

Week 2

O Morning Star, O radiant Sun,
when will our hearts behold your dawn?
O Sun, arise; without your light
we grope in gloom and dark of night.

> Text: *German spiritual song; tr. Martin L. Seltz*
> Tune: *OLD HUNDREDTH (Praise God from whom all blessings flow) or TALLIS' CANON*

Oh, come, oh, come, Emmanuel

Week 3

Oh, come, oh, come, Emmanuel,
and ransom captive Israel,
that mourns in lonely exile here
until the Son of God appear.
    Rejoice! Rejoice!
    Emmanuel shall come to you, O Israel.

Week 4

Oh, come, blest Dayspring, come and cheer
our spirits by your advent here;
disperse the gloomy clouds of night,
and death's dark shadows put to flight.
    Rejoice! Rejoice!
    Emmanuel shall come to you, O Israel.

> Text: *Psalteriolum Cantionum Catholicarum; tr. John Neale*
> Tune: *VENI, EMMANUEL*

CHRISTMAS

The lighting of a white candle may begin daily prayer.

A carol for Christmas

What child is this

What child is this, who, laid to rest, on Mary's lap is sleeping?
Whom angels greet with anthems sweet
while shepherds watch are keeping?
This, this is Christ the king,
whom shepherds guard and angels sing;
haste, haste to bring him laud, the babe, the son of Mary!

Why lies he in such mean estate where ox and ass are feeding?
Good Christian, fear; for sinners here
the silent Word is pleading.
Nails, spear shall pierce him through,
the cross be borne for me, for you;
hail, hail the Word made flesh, the babe, the son of Mary!

So bring him incense, gold, and myrrh;
come, peasant, king, to own him.
The King of kings salvation brings;
let loving hearts enthrone him.
Raise, raise the song on high, the virgin sings her lullaby;
joy, joy, for Christ is born, the babe, the son of Mary!

> *Text: William Dix*
> *Tune: GREENSLEEVES*

A psalm for Christmas

In the beauty of holiness have I begotten you,
like the dew from the womb of the morning.   *Psalm 110:3*

Sing to the LORD a new song,
> for the LORD has done marvelous things.

The right hand and the holy arm of the LORD
> have secured the victory.

The LORD has made known this victory
> and has openly shown righteousness in the sight of the
> > nations.

The LORD remembers mercy and faithfulness to the house
> of Israel,
> and all the ends of the earth have seen the victory of our
> > God.

Shout with joy to the LORD, all you lands;
> lift up your voice, rejoice, and sing.

Sing to the LORD with the harp,
> with the harp and the voice of song.

With trumpets and the sound of the horn
> shout with joy before the Sovereign, the LORD.

Let the sea make a noise and all that is in it,
> the lands and those who dwell therein.

Let the rivers clap their hands,
> and let the hills ring out with joy before the LORD,
> who is coming to judge the earth.

In righteousness shall the LORD judge the world
> and the peoples with equity.   *Psalm 98*

Readings for Christmas

See the daily readings

A canticle for Christmas

Today Christ is born; today salvation has appeared.
Today the just exult and say, Glory to God in the highest.
Alleluia.

Morning: The Song of Zechariah
Evening: The Song of Mary
Bedtime: The Song of Simeon

or

Glory to God in the highest,
and peace to God's people on earth.

Lord God, heavenly King,
almighty God and Father,
   we worship you, we give you thanks,
   we praise you for your glory.

Lord Jesus Christ, only Son of the Father,
Lord God, Lamb of God,
you take away the sin of the world:
   have mercy on us;
you are seated at the right hand of the Father:
   receive our prayer.

For you alone are the Holy One,
you alone are the Lord,
you alone are the Most High,
   Jesus Christ,
   with the Holy Spirit,
   in the glory of God the Father. Amen.
    Gloria in excelsis Deo (Luke 2:14 with acclamations)

A prayer for Christmas

Almighty God,
you wonderfully created and yet more wonderfully restored
the dignity of human nature.
In your mercy, let us share the divine life of Jesus Christ
who came to share our humanity,
and who now lives and reigns with you and the Holy Spirit,
one God, now and forever.
Amen.

Christmas table prayer

Glory to God in the highest!
Peace to God's people on earth!
To you is born this day a Savior, who is Christ the Lord.
O come, let us worship him.

With joy and gladness
we feast upon your love, O God.
You have come among us in Jesus, your Son,
and your presence now graces this table.
May Christ dwell in us
that we might bear his love to all the world,
for he is Lord forever and ever.
Amen.

DAILY READINGS AND PRAYERS

Christmas Day

December 25	Isa. 52:7-20	Ps. 98
	Heb. 1:1-4	John 1:1-14
December 26	Luke 2:1-20	
December 27	Isa. 62:6-12	
December 28	Ps. 96	
December 29	Gen. 1:1—2:4a	
December 30	Ps. 97	
December 31	Titus 2:11—3:7	

For prayer throughout the day
The Word lives among us. Alleluia.　　*See John 1:14*

A prayer for the days after Christmas
Almighty God,
you enlighten the darkness with the true Light.
In the days ahead, help us walk in Christ's light,
and on the last day awaken us to the brightness of his glory.
Amen.

First Sunday after Christmas

S	Isa. 63:7-9	Ps. 148
	Heb. 2:10-18	Matt. 2:13-23
M	Hosea 11:1-11	
T	Jer. 31:15-22	
W	Matt. 13:54-58	
Th	Isa. 61:10—62:3	
F	Exod. 1:15—2:10	
S	Ps. 147	

For prayer throughout the day
Lord, I put my trust in you.   *See Hebrews 2:13*

A prayer for the week
Lord Jesus,
we are your brothers and sisters.
Hear us when we call to you.
Come to our aid.
Amen.

Second Sunday after Christmas

S   Jer. 31:7-14   Ps. 147:12-20
      Eph. 1:3-14   John 1:10-18

For prayer throughout the day
O Christ, draw us close to God's heart.   *See John 1:18*

A prayer for the week
God our creator,
you have filled us with the light of the Word made flesh.
Let the light of our faith so shine in our lives
that others may give praise to you.
Amen.

BLESSING OF THE CHRISTMAS TREE

Whether you live alone or with others, this prayer may be said after the tree is decorated and before the lights are first shining, or on Christmas Eve/Day. If present, an older child may read the scripture text.

Invitation

Let us praise Christ
who brings us God's mercy and peace,
now and forever.
Amen.

Reading

As we prepare for the celebration of Christmas,
let us listen to the words of scripture:

A shoot shall come out from the stump of Jesse,
   and a branch shall grow out of his roots.
The spirit of the LORD shall rest on him,
   the spirit of wisdom and understanding,
   the spirit of counsel and might,
   the spirit of knowledge and the fear of the LORD.

The root of Jesse shall stand as a signal to the peoples; the nations shall inquire of him, and his dwelling shall be glorious. *Isaiah 11:1-2, 10*

Prayer of blessing

Let us pray.

God our Creator,
we praise you for this Christmas tree.
It is a sign of your everlasting, evergreen presence.
It is a sign of the reign of heaven,
sheltering the creatures of the earth under its open arms.
It is a sign of the cross,
shining with the light of your grace and mercy.

Gracious God,
let your blessing come upon us
as we illumine this tree.
Send us your Son,
the tender shoot of Jesse,
who brings us light and life.
May all who stand in its light
eagerly welcome the true Light which never fades.
We ask this through Christ our Lord.
Amen.

Song

Oh, come, oh, come, Emmanuel

Oh, come, strong Branch of Jesse, free
your own from Satan's tyranny;
from depths of hell your people save
and give them vict'ry over the grave.
   Rejoice! Rejoice!
   Emmanuel shall come to you, O Israel.
     Text: Psalteriolum Cantionum Catholicarum; tr. John Neale
     Tune: VENI, EMMANUEL

BLESSING OF THE NATIVITY SCENE

Whether you live alone or with others, this prayer may be used when a nativity scene is placed in the home, on Christmas Eve/Day, or on one of the days of Christmas. If present, young children may place the figures in the creche before the blessing. It is the custom in some homes to place the infant in the manger on Christmas Eve/Day and add the Magi on the feast of the Epiphany. An older child may read the scripture text.

Invitation

Let us praise Christ
who brings light to the homes of all believers
now and forever.
Amen.

Reading

As we celebrate the birth of Christ in a humble dwelling,
let us listen to the words of scripture:

In those days a decree went out from Emperor Augustus that all the world should be registered. This was the first registration and was taken while Quirinius was governor of Syria. All went to their own towns to be registered. Joseph also went from the town of Nazareth in Galilee to Judea, to the city of David called Bethlehem, because he was descended from the house and family of David. He went to be registered with Mary, to whom he was engaged and who was expecting a child. While they were there, the time came for her to deliver her child. And she gave birth to her firstborn son and wrapped him in bands of cloth, and laid him in a manger, because there was no place for them in the inn.   *Luke 2:1-7*

Prayer of blessing

Let us pray.

Blessed are you, O Lord our God,
ruler of the universe.
With Mary and Joseph,
with the angels and the shepherds,
and with the animals in the stable
we gather around your Son, born for us.
Bless us, and fill us with joy and wonder
as we look upon this manger scene.
Inspire us to care for those who have no place to dwell:
the migrant worker, the homeless, the refugee.
Be with us that we might share Christ's love
with all the world,
for he is our light and our salvation.
Blessed be God forever.

Song

Away in a Manger

Away in a manger, no crib for his bed,
the little Lord Jesus laid down his sweet head;
the stars in the sky looked down where he lay,
the little Lord Jesus asleep on the hay.
    Text and tune: American, 19th cent.

Go tell it on the mountain

Refrain:

Go tell it on the mountain, over the hills and ev'rywhere;
go tell it on the mountain that Jesus Christ is born!

Down in a lonely manger the humble Christ was born;
and God sent us salvation that blessed Christmas morn. *Refrain*

Text: African American spiritual, refrain; John W. Work Jr., stanza
Tune: African American spiritual

BLESSING OF GIFTS

Many people exchange and open gifts on Christmas Eve or Christmas Day. Others open gifts on the Epiphany, January 6, which celebrates the Magi bringing gifts to the newborn Christ. Still others keep the Twelve Days from Christmas to Epiphany, by opening a gift each night. Whether you live alone or with others, this prayer may be used before the opening of gifts.

Invitation

Let us praise Christ
who brings us the gift of salvation
now and forever.
Amen.

Reading

As we prepare to open these gifts,
let us listen to the words of scripture:

The wise men set out; and there, ahead of them, went the star that they had seen at its rising, until it stopped over the place where the child was. When they saw that the star had stopped, they were overwhelmed with joy. On entering the house, they saw the child with Mary his mother; and they knelt down and paid him homage. Then, opening their treasure chests, they offered him gifts of gold, frankincense, and myrrh.
Matthew 2:9-11

Prayer of blessing

Let us pray.

Blessed be your name, O God,
you are the source of every blessing.
From your hand, we receive the good gifts
of life, health, and salvation.
As we give and receive these presents,
bless us with hearts thankful for the birth of your Son.
May our opening of these gifts lead us
to share our love, faith, and goods with the poor and needy.
Blessed be God forever.

Song

We three kings

We three kings of Orient are,
bearing gifts we traverse afar,
field and fountain, moor and mountain,
following yonder star.
Refrain: O star of wonder, star of night,
    star with royal beauty bright;
    westward leading, still proceeding,
    guide us to thy perfect light!

Glorious now behold him arise,
King and God and sacrifice;
Heav'n sings, "alleluia";
"Alleluia," earth replies. *Refrain*
    Text and tune: John Henry Hopkins Jr.

If this blessing is used on Christmas Eve:

Noche de paz

¡Noche de paz; noche de_amor!
Todo duerme_en derredor.
Entre los astros que_esparsen su luz,
bella,_anunciando_al niñito Jesús,
   brilla la_estrella de paz;
   brilla la_estrella de paz.

¡Noche de paz; noche de_amor!
Ved qúe bello resplandor
luce_en el rostro de niño Jesús:
en el pesebre, del mundo la luz,
   astro de_eterno fulgor;
   astro de_eterno fulgor.

Text: Joseph Mohr; tr. Federico Fliedner
Tune: STILLE NACHT (Silent Night), Franz X. Gruber

CHRISTMASTIME: THE TWELVE DAYS

Christians celebrate the Nativity of the Lord between Christmas (December 25) and the Epiphany (January 6)—twelve days of exchanging gifts, gathering at the Christmas tree for prayer, lighting candles by the nativity scene, reading from scripture, and singing Christmas carols and hymns.

Since the fourth century, the church has commemorated the "companions of Christ," those who followed the Savior as disciples and martyrs.

December 26   Stephen, Deacon and Martyr

Matthew 23:34-39

Grant us grace, O Lord,
that like Stephen we may learn to love even our enemies
and seek forgiveness for those who desire our hurt;
through your Son, Jesus Christ our Lord,
who lives and reigns with you and the Holy Spirit,
one God, now and forever.
Amen.

December 27   John, Apostle and Evangelist

John 21:20-25

Merciful Lord,
let the brightness of your light shine on your church,
so that all of us,
instructed by the teachings of John,
your apostle and evangelist,

may walk in the light of your truth and attain eternal life;
through your Son, Jesus Christ our Lord,
who lives and reigns with you and the Holy Spirit,
one God, now and forever.
Amen.

December 28   The Holy Innocents, Martyrs

Matthew 2:13-18

We remember today, O God,
the slaughter of the holy innocents of Bethlehem
by the order of King Herod.
Receive, we pray, into the arms of your mercy
all innocent victims,
and by your great might frustrate the designs of evil tyrants
and establish your rule of justice, love, and peace;
through Jesus Christ our Lord,
who lives and reigns with you and the Holy Spirit,
one God, now and forever.
Amen.

December 31   New Year's Eve

Luke 13:6-9

Eternal Father,
you have placed us in a world of space and time,
and through the events of our lives
you bless us with your love.
Grant that in this new year
we may know your presence,
see your love at work,
and live in the light of the event which gives us joy forever—

the coming of your Son, Jesus Christ our Lord.
Amen.

*Eight days after Christmas, many Christians celebrate the
day on which Jesus was given his name according to Jewish
practice.*

January 1   The Name of Jesus

Luke 2:15-21

Eternal Father,
you gave your Son the name of Jesus
to be a sign of our salvation.
Plant in every heart
the love of the Savior of the world,
Jesus Christ our Lord,
who lives and reigns with you and the Holy Spirit,
one God, now and forever.
Amen.

December 26–January 1   Kwanzaa

Kwanzaa is an African American celebration of the family
and its African heritage. Between December 26 and New
Year's Day, many African Americans keep Kwanzaa with
prayer, the lighting of the *Kinara* (a seven-branched candle
holder), reflection on the *Nguzo Saba* (seven principles of
African heritage), the sharing of *Kikombe* (a unity cup), festive
meals, and the giving of *zawadi* (gifts) to children.

EPIPHANY

The lighting of a candle may begin daily prayer.

A hymn for Epiphany

When Christ's appearing was made known,

When Christ's appearing was made known,
King Herod trembled for his throne;
but he who offers heav'nly birth
seeks not the kingdoms of this earth.

The eastern sages saw from far
and followed on his guiding star;
by light their way to light they trod,
and by their gifts confessed their God.

Within the Jordan's sacred flood
the heav'nly Lamb in meekness stood,
that he, of whom no sin was known,
might cleanse his people from their own.

And oh, what miracle divine,
when water reddened into wine!
He spoke the word, and forth it flowed
in streams that nature ne'er bestowed.

For this his glad epiphany,
all glory unto Jesus be:
Whom with the Father we adore,
and Holy Ghost forevermore.

> *Text: Coelius Sedulius, 5th cent.; tr. John Neale et al.*
> *Tune: WO GOTT ZUM HAUS or HER KOMMER DINE ARME SMAA*
> *(Your little ones, dear Lord, are we) or TALLIS' CANON*

A psalm for Epiphany

With joy you will draw water from the wells of salvation.
   Isaiah 12:3

Give the king your justice, O God,
   and your righteousness to a king's son.
May he judge your people with righteousness,
   and your poor with justice.
May the mountains yield prosperity for the people,
   and the hills, in righteousness.
May he defend the cause of the poor of the people,
   give deliverance to the needy,
   and crush the oppressor.

May he live while the sun endures,
   and as long as the moon, throughout all generations.
May he be like rain that falls on the mown grass,
   like showers that water the earth.
In his days may righteousness flourish
   and peace abound, until the moon is no more.

May he have dominion from sea to sea,
   and from the River to the ends of the earth.
May his foes bow down before him,
   and his enemies lick the dust.
May the kings of Tarshish and of the isles
   render him tribute,
may the Kings of Sheba and Saba
   bring gifts.
may all kings fall down before him,
   all nations give him service.

For he delivers the needy when they call,
   the poor and those who have no helper.
He has pity on the weak and the needy,
   and saves the lives of the needy.

From oppression and violence he redeems their life;
    and precious is their blood in his sight.

Long may he live! *Psalm 72:1-15a*

Readings for Epiphany

See the daily readings

A canticle for Epiphany

Today the star leads the Magi to the infant redeemer;
today Christ is baptized by John in the River Jordan;
today water is changed to wine for the wedding feast at Cana.

Morning: The Song of Zechariah
Evening: The Song of Mary
Bedtime: The Song of Simeon

or

Arise, shine; for your light has come,
    and the glory of the LORD has risen upon you.
For darkness shall cover the earth,
    and thick darkness the peoples;
but the LORD will arise upon you,
    and his glory will appear over you.
Nations shall come to your light,
    and kings to the brightness of your dawn.

Violence shall no more be heard in your land,
    devastation or destruction within your borders;
you shall call your walls Salvation,
    and your gates Praise.

The sun shall no longer be
    your light by day,

nor for brightness shall the moon
    give light to you by night;
but the LORD will be your everlasting light,
    and your God will be your glory.
        Isaiah 60:1-3, 18-19

Prayers for Epiphany

Lord God,
on this day you revealed your Son to the nations
by the leading of a star.
Lead us now by faith to know your presence in our lives,
and bring us at last to the full vision of your glory,
through your Son, Jesus Christ our Lord,
who lives and reigns with you and the Holy Spirit,
one God, now and forever.
Amen.

Father in heaven,
at the baptism of Jesus in the River Jordan
you proclaimed him your beloved Son
and anointed him with the Holy Spirit.
Make all who are baptized into Christ
faithful in their calling to be your children
and inheritors with him of everlasting life;
through your Son, Jesus Christ our Lord,
who lives and reigns with you and the Holy Spirit,
one God, now and forever.
Amen.

Epiphany table prayer

Arise, shine; for your light has come.
The glory of the Lord has risen upon you.
Nations shall come to your light,
and rulers to the brightness of your dawn.

Generous God,
you have made yourself known in Jesus, the light of the world.
As this food and drink give us refreshment,
so strengthen us by your Spirit,
that as your baptized sons and daughters
we may share your light with all the world.
Grant this through Christ our Lord.
Amen.

DAILY READINGS AND PRAYERS

Epiphany of the Lord

Jan 6	Isa. 60:1-6	Ps. 72:1-7, 10-14
	Eph. 3:1-12	Matt. 2:1-12
Jan 7	1 Kings 10:1-10	
Jan 8	1 Kings 10:14-25	
Jan 9	John 18:33—19:22	
Jan 10	Micah 5:1-9	
Jan 11	Eph. 3:14-21	
Jan 12	Ps. 97	

For prayer throughout the day
Jesus, bright star, be with me.

A prayer for the week
Lord Jesus,
you have given us many good gifts.
May our words of peace and acts of justice
shed light in the darkness.
Amen.

Baptism of the Lord

S	Isa. 42:1-9	Ps. 29
	Acts 10:34-43	Matt. 3:13-17
M	2 Sam. 23:1-7	
T	Jer. 1:4-10	
W	Matt. 12:9-21	
Th	Isa. 51:7-16	
F	Acts 10:1-48	
S	Ps. 89:1-37	

For prayer throughout the day
Servant of God, wash us in your mercy.

A prayer for the week
Mothering God,
you have given us birth in the waters of baptism.
May your Spirit strengthen us
to be your witnesses.
Amen.

Second Sunday after the Epiphany

S	Isa. 49:1-7	Ps. 40:1-11
	1 Cor. 1:1-9	John 1:29-42
M	Exod. 12:1-28	
T	Isa. 53:1-12	
W	Matt. 9:14-17	
Th	Isa. 48:12-21	
F	Acts 8:26-40	
S	Ps. 40	

For prayer throughout the day
Holy One, give us your light.

A prayer for the week
O God,
make us strong in every spiritual gift
so that we may serve you with confidence.
Amen.

Third Sunday after the Epiphany

S	Isa. 9:1-4	Ps. 27:1,4-9
	1 Cor. 1:10-18	Matt. 4:12-23

M	Exod. 3:1-20		
T	Judg. 6:1-24		
W	Matt. 4:23-25		
Th	Judg. 7:15-25		
F	Luke 1:67-79		
S	Ps. 27		

For prayer throughout the day
The LORD is my light and my salvation.   *Psalm 27:1*

A prayer for the week
God our Savior,
as you called the first disciples,
be with us now when we invite others
to walk on the path to your kingdom.
Amen.

Fourth Sunday after the Epiphany

S	Micah 6:1-8	Ps. 15	
	1 Cor. 1:18-31	Matt. 5:1-12	
M	Ruth 1:1—2:13		
T	Ruth 4:1-22		
W	Luke 6:17-26		
Th	Zeph. 2:3; 3:12-13		
F	Philemon		
S	Ps. 37:1-17		

For prayer throughout the day
Blessed are the merciful.   *Matthew 5:7*

A prayer for the week
O God,
you ask us to do justice,
to love kindness, and to walk with you in humility
Give us the strength to do what is good.
Amen.

Fifth Sunday after the Epiphany

S	Isa. 58:1-9a	Ps. 112:1-9
	1 Cor. 2:1-12	Matt. 5:13-20
M	2 Kings 22:1-20	
T	2 Kings 23:1-25	
W	John 8:12-30	
Th	Heb. 3:1-4, 17-19	
F	2 Cor. 4:1-12	
S	Ps. 112	

For prayer throughout the day
Lord Jesus, teach me your wisdom.

A prayer for the week
Gracious God,
you have given us the light of your abundant truth.
May we share its riches with all who seek the truth.
Amen.

Sixth Sunday after the Epiphany

S	Deut. 30:15-20	Ps. 119:1-8
	1 Cor. 3:1-9	Matt. 5:21-37
M	Exod. 20:1-21	
T	Deut. 23:21—24:18	
W	John 8:1-11	
Th	Prov. 2:1-15	

F   James 2:1-13
S   Ps. 119:17-32

For prayer throughout the day
Jesus, Mercy, lead me in the path of life.   *See Psalm 119:1*

A prayer for the week
O God,
you walk with us each day.
In the midst of fear and death
help us to follow the path of hope and life.
Amen.

Seventh Sunday after the Epiphany

S   Lev. 19:1-2, 9-18   Ps. 119:33-40
        1 Cor. 3:10-11, 16-23   Matt. 5:38-48
M   Lev. 24:10-23
T   Gen. 4:1-16
W   Matt. 7:12-20
Th   Prov. 25:11-23
F   Rom. 12:9-21
S   Ps. 119:41-56

For prayer throughout the day
God my Rock, be my strength this day.
    See 1 Corinthians 3:11

A prayer for the week
Heavenly Father,
teach us holy wisdom:
to love our enemies,
to welcome strangers,
to return good for evil.
Amen.

Eighth Sunday after the Epiphany

S	Isa. 49:8-16a	Ps. 131
	1 Cor. 4:1-5	Matt. 6:24-34
M	Deut. 32:1-14	
T	1 Kings 17:1-16	
W	Luke 12:22-31	
Th	Isa. 66:7-14	
F	Phil. 4:4-13	
S	Ps. 104:10-28	

For prayer throughout the day
O God, hold me in the palm of your hand.   *See Isaiah 49:16*

A prayer for the week
Provident God,
when we worry ourselves into knots,
untangle us with the gentle hands of your mercy.
May we trust your ever-present care.
Amen.

Transfiguration

S	Exod. 24:12-18	Ps. 2
	2 Peter 1:16-21	Matt. 17:1-9
M	Exod. 33:7-23	
T	1 Kings 19:1-3, 9-18	

For prayer throughout the day
Christ, morning star, fill our hearts with your love.

A prayer for the week
O God,
in the transfiguration of your Son
we see your gracious light.
Give us the grace to live as children of the light.
Amen.

BLESSING OF THE HOUSEHOLD AT EPIPHANY

Matthew writes that when the wise men saw the shining star stop overhead, they were filled with joy. "On entering the house, they saw the child with Mary his mother" (2:11). In the home, Christ is met in family and friends, in visitors and strangers. In the home faith is shared, nurtured, and put into action. In the home, Christ is welcome.

Whether you live alone or with others, you may invite friends and other family members to gather for this blessing, followed by refreshments or a festive meal. Someone may lead with the greeting and blessing while someone else may read the scripture reading.

Invitation

May the peace of the Word made flesh be with us
and with all who enter here.
Amen.

By wisdom a house is built,
    and by understanding it is established;
by knowledge its rooms are filled
    with all precious and pleasant riches.   *Proverbs 24:3-4*

Reading

As we prepare to ask God's blessing on this household,
let us listen to the words of scripture.

In the beginning was the Word, and the Word was with God, and the Word was God. He was in the beginning with God. All things came into being through him, and without him not one thing came into being. What has come into being in him was life, and the life was the light of all people.

The Word became flesh and lived among us, and we have seen his glory, the glory as of a father's only son, full of grace and truth. From his fullness we have all received, grace upon grace.   *John 1:1-4, 14, 16*

Prayer of blessing

Let us pray.

O God,
you revealed your Son to all people
by the shining light of a star.

We pray that you bless this home and *those* who *live* here
with your gracious presence.
May your love be *their* inspiration,
your wisdom *their* guide,
your truth *their* light,
and your peace *their* benediction;
through Jesus Christ our Lord.
Amen.

The Lord's Prayer

Song

As with gladness men of old

As with gladness men of old
did the guiding star behold;
as with joy they hailed its light,
leading onward, beaming bright;
so, most gracious Lord, may we
evermore be led by thee.

In the heav'nly country bright
need they no created light;
thou its light, its joy, its crown,
thou its sun which goes not down;
there forever may we sing
alleluias to our King.
  Text: William Dix
  Tune: DIX

CHRISTIAN UNITY

Between January 18 and January 25, many Christians keep the Week of Prayer for Christian Unity. In the home, at church, and in ecumenical prayer services, the unity that Christians share through baptism may be the focus of prayer and reflection.

January 18   The Confession of St. Peter

Acts 4:8-13   Ps. 18:1-7,17-20   1 Cor. 10:1-5   Matt. 16:13-19

Almighty God,
you inspired Simon Peter to confess Jesus
as the Messiah and Son of the living God.
Keep your church firm on the rock of this faith,
that in unity and peace
it may proclaim one truth and follow one Lord,
your Son, our Savior Jesus Christ,
who lives and reigns with you and the Holy Spirit,
one God, now and forever.
Amen.

The unity of the church

Isa. 2:2-4   Ps. 133   Eph. 4:1-6   John 17:15-23

God our Father,
your Son Jesus prayed that his followers might be one.
Make all Christians one with him as he is one with you,
so that in peace and concord we may carry to the world
the message of your love;
through your Son, Jesus Christ our Lord,
who lives and reigns with you and the Holy Spirit,
one God, now and forever.
Amen.

January 25   The Conversion of St. Paul

Acts 9:1-22   Ps. 67   Gal. 1:11-24   Luke 21:10-19

Lord God,
through the preaching of your apostle Paul,
you established one church from among the nations.
As we celebrate his conversion,
we pray that we may follow his example
and be witnesses to the truth in your Son,
Jesus Christ our Lord,
who lives and reigns with you and the Holy Spirit,
one God, now and forever.

Lent • The Three Days • Easter

Lent is a forty-day journey to Easter. Christians keep company with Noah and his family, who were in the ark for forty days; with the Hebrews, who journeyed through the desert for forty years; and with Moses, Elijah, and Jesus, who fasted for forty days before they embarked on the tasks God had prepared for them.

During Lent Christians journey with those who are making final preparations for baptism at Easter. Together, Christians struggle with the meaning of their baptismal promises: Do you reject evil? Do you believe in God the Father, the Son, and the Holy Spirit? Do you believe in the church, the forgiveness of sins, the resurrection of the dead?

The disciples of the Lord Jesus are called to struggle against everything that leads away from love of God and neighbor. Fasting, prayer, and works of love—the disciplines of Lent—help the household rejoice in the gifts of baptism: God's forgiveness and mercy.

The word *Lent* means "lengthen." With longer days and spring in sight, Christians move toward the goal of the Lenten journey: the celebration of the Lord's death and resurrection at Easter.

During the Three Days of Holy Week (Maundy/Holy Thursday, Good Friday, Holy Saturday/Easter Sunday), Christians celebrate the events of Jesus' passion, death, and resurrection. In public worship, Christians celebrate the washing of feet and the Lord's Supper on Maundy/Holy Thursday, the victory of the cross on Good Friday, the presence of God's light and salvation in the risen Christ on Holy Saturday/Easter Sunday. The ancient Christian name for the Three Days is the Paschal Triduum, *paschal* referring to Jesus' "pasch" or passover from death to risen life, and *triduum* referring to the "three days."

As the sun sets on Maundy/Holy Thursday, so Lent ends and the Three Days begin, ending with sunset on Easter Day. During these central days, Christians prepare to celebrate God's gift of new life given in baptism. Indeed, the readings of the Three Days move toward the baptismal font where new brothers and sisters are born of water and the Spirit, and where the baptized renew their baptismal promises.

The Three Days flow into the rejoicing of the Fifty Days of Easter. During this "week of weeks," Christians explore the meaning of the central actions of baptism for daily life: the renouncing of evil and the professing of faith, washing in water, being marked with the cross, clothing in the white robe, receiving the light of the paschal/Easter candle, and eating and drinking the bread of life and the cup of salvation.

The Fifty Days were once called *Pentecost*, Greek for "fifty." On the fiftieth day of Easter, Christians celebrate the pentecostal mystery of the risen Christ breathing on the church the breath, the wind, and the fire of the Holy Spirit.

From the ashes of Lent to the fire and wind of Pentecost, the church heeds this invitation: Come to the feast! Come to the feast of bright light, refreshing waters, and a welcome table!

LENT

ASH WEDNESDAY

From Ash Wednesday to Pentecost Sunday, a place in the home may be set aside for prayer. A small bowl of water may be placed there with a candle, a cross or crucifix, and a Bible. From Ash Wednesday until the Easter Vigil, the joyful Alleluia is not sung or spoken in prayer.

Prayer

Almighty and ever-living God,
you hate nothing you have made
and you forgive the sins of all who are penitent.
Create in us new and honest hearts,
so that, truly repenting of our sins,
we may obtain from you, the God of all mercy,
full pardon and forgiveness;
through your Son, Jesus Christ our Lord,
who lives and reigns with you and the Holy Spirit,
one God, now and forever.
Amen.

Reading

Is such the fast that I choose,
   a day to humble oneself?
Is it to bow down the head like a bulrush,
   and to lie in sackcloth and ashes?
Will you call this a fast,
   a day acceptable to the LORD?

Is not this the fast that I choose:
   to loose the bonds of injustice,
   to undo the thongs of the yoke,
to let the oppressed go free,
   and to break every yoke?
Is it not to share your bread with the hungry,
   and bring the homeless poor into your house;
when you see the naked, to cover them,
   and not to hide yourself from your own kin?
Then your light shall break forth like the dawn,
   and your healing shall spring up quickly;
your vindicator shall go before you,
   the glory of the LORD shall be your rear guard.
Then you shall call, and the LORD will answer;
   you shall cry for help, and he will say, Here I am.

If you remove the yoke from among you,
   the pointing of the finger, the speaking of evil,
if you offer your food to the hungry
   and satisfy the needs of the afflicted,
then your light shall rise in the darkness
   and your gloom be like the noonday.   *Isaiah 58:5-10*

Prayer of blessing

Let us pray.

Merciful God,
you formed us out of the dust of the earth;
you made us brothers and sisters of Christ
in the waters of holy baptism;
you feed us with your Word,
the bread of life and the cup of blessing.

Look with mercy upon us as we begin these Forty Days,
marked with the cross of Christ.
Guide us on our journey through the desert of Lent
to the refreshing waters of Easter's font.

May our fasting deepen our hunger for justice.
May our prayer open us to your gracious presence.
May our works of love enlarge our desire
to serve the poor and needy.

We ask this through our Lord Jesus Christ,
who lives and reigns with you and the Holy Spirit,
one God, now and forever.
Amen.

THE LENTEN SEASON

A hymn for Lent

As the sun with longer journey

As the sun with longer journey melts the winter's snow and ice,
with its slowly growing radiance
   warms the seed beneath the earth,
may the sun of Christ's uprising gently bring our hearts to life.

Through the days of waiting, watching, in the desert of our sin,
searching on the far horizon for a sign of cloud or wind,
we await the healing waters of our Savior's victory.

Praise be given to the maker of the seasons' yearly round:
Father, Son, and Holy Spirit—Source, Sustainer, Lord of life,
as the ever turning ages roll to their eternal rest.
    Text: John Patrick Earls, O.S.B.
    Tune: PRAISE, MY SOUL (Praise my soul, the King of heaven) or
    PICARDY (Let all mortal flesh keep silence)

A psalm for Lent

I will sprinkle clean water upon you, and you shall be clean.
A new heart I will give you,
and a new spirit I will put within you.   *Ezekiel 36:25a, 26a*

Have mercy on me, O God,
   according to your steadfast love;
according to your abundant mercy
   blot out my transgressions.
Wash me thoroughly from my iniquity,
   and cleanse me from my sin.

For I know my transgressions,
   and my sin is ever before me.

Against you, you alone, have I sinned,
    and done what is evil in your sight,
so that you are justified in your sentence
    and blameless when you pass judgment.
Indeed, I was born guilty,
    a sinner when my mother conceived me.

You desire truth in the inward being;
    therefore teach me wisdom in my secret heart.
Purge me with hyssop, and I shall be clean;
    wash me, and I shall be whiter than snow.
Let me hear joy and gladness;
    let the bones that you have crushed rejoice.
Hide your face from my sins,
    and blot out all my iniquities.

Create in me a clean heart, O God,
    and put a new and right spirit within me.
Do not cast me away from your presence,
    and do not take your holy spirit from me.
Restore to me the joy of your salvation,
    and sustain in me a willing spirit.

Then I will teach transgressors your ways,
    and sinners will return to you.   *Psalm 51:1-13*

Readings for Lent

See the daily readings

A canticle for Lent

God so loved the world that he gave his only Son,
so that everyone who believes in him may not perish
but may have eternal life.   *John 3:16*

Morning: The Song of Zechariah
Evening: The Song of Mary
Bedtime: The Song of Simeon

or

Seek the LORD while he may be found,
   call upon him while he is near;
let the wicked forsake their way,
   and the unrighteous their thoughts;
let them return to the LORD, that he may have mercy on
         them,
   and to our God, for he will abundantly pardon.

For my thoughts are not your thoughts,
   nor are your ways my ways, says the LORD.
For as the heavens are higher than the earth,
   so are my ways higher than your ways
   and my thoughts than your thoughts.

For as the rain and the snow come down from heaven,
   and do not return there until they have watered the earth,
making it bring forth and sprout,
   giving seed to the sower and bread to the eater,
so shall my word be that goes out from my mouth;
   it shall not return to me empty,
but it shall accomplish that which I purpose,
   and succeed in the thing for which I sent it.
      Isaiah 55:6-11

A prayer for Lent

O Lord God,
you led your ancient people through the barren desert
and brought them to the promised land.
Guide us now as we follow our Savior
through the wilderness of Lent
to the life-giving waters of Easter.
Keep us faithful to your Word
and strengthen our trust in your mercy.
Grant this through Christ our Lord.
Amen.

Lent table prayer

Behold, now is the acceptable time.
Now is the day of salvation.
In peace, let us pray to the Lord.
Lord, have mercy.

Blessed are you, O Lord our God, maker of all things.
Through your goodness you have blessed us
with the gifts of this table.
Turn our hearts toward you,
and toward all those in need.
May our Lenten journey bring us to the rebirth of Easter,
through Christ our Lord.
Amen.

DAILY READINGS AND PRAYERS

Ash Wednesday   Joel 2:1-2, 12-17   Ps. 51:1-17
                    2 Cor. 5:20b—6:10   Matt. 6:1-6, 16-21
        Th   Jonah 3:1-10
         F   Jonah 4:1-11
         S   Isa. 58:1-12

For prayer throughout the day
Return to the LORD, your God.   *Joel 2:13*

A prayer for the week
Have mercy on me, O God,
according to your steadfast love;
wash me thoroughly from my iniquity,
and cleanse me from my sin.
Amen.

First Sunday in Lent

S   Gen. 2:15-17; 3:1-7   Ps. 32
         Rom. 5:12-19   Matt. 4:1-11
M   Exod. 34:1-28
T   1 Kings 19:1-8
W   Matt. 18:21-28
Th   Exod. 23:20-33
F   Heb. 4:14—5:14
S   Ps. 38

For prayer throughout the day
O God, you are a hiding place for me.   *Psalm 32:7*

A prayer for the week
Lord God,
keep us steadfast in your Word.
When we fall, raise us again and restore us
through your Son, Jesus Christ our Lord.
Amen.

Second Sunday in Lent

S	Gen. 12:1-4a	Ps. 121
	Rom. 4:1-5, 13-17	John 3:1-17
M	Isa. 65:17-25	
T	Ezek. 36:22-32	
W	Luke 1:5-25	
Th	Num. 21:4-9	
F	Rom. 4:13-25	
S	Ps. 128	

For prayer throughout the day
My help comes from the LORD.   *Psalm 121:2*

A prayer for the week
Ever-watchful God,
keep my feet from stumbling,
guard me from all evil,
and protect me from the burning sun.
Amen.

Third Sunday in Lent

S	Exod. 17:1-7	Ps. 95	
	Rom. 5:1-11	John 4:5-42	
M	Gen. 24:1-27		
T	Gen. 24:28-67		
W	John 7:14-39		
Th	Jer. 2:1-13		
F	1 John 5:1-13		
S	Ps. 96		

For prayer throughout the day
Pour your love into our hearts, O God.   *See Romans 5:5*

A prayer for the week
O God,
we thirst for the water of life.
In your mercy, refresh us with the life-giving streams
of your Word and sacraments.
Amen.

Fourth Sunday in Lent

S	1 Sam. 16:1-13	Ps. 23	
	Eph. 5:8-14	John 9:1-41	
M	Isa. 29:9-22		
T	Isa. 59:9-19		
W	Matt. 9:27—10:4		
Th	Isa. 42:5-21		
F	Acts 9:1-20		
S	Ps. 146		

For prayer throughout the day
Help us walk as children of the light.   *See Ephesians 5:8*

A prayer for the week
O God,
open our eyes
so that we may see your gracious presence
in the ordinary events of everyday life.
Amen.

Fifth Sunday in Lent

S	Ezek. 37:1-14	Ps. 130
	Rom. 8:6-11	John 11:1-45
M	1 Kings 17:8-24	
T	2 Kings 4:8-37	
W	John 12:12-26	
Th	Jer. 32:1-15, 27-41	
F	Eph. 2:1-10	
S	Ps. 142	

For prayer throughout the day
Lord Jesus, you are the resurrection and the life.
See John 11:25

A prayer for the week
O God,
with you there is steadfast love
and the power to save us from final darkness.
May we live as servants of your mercy
and children of your gracious light.
Amen.

Holy Week

On the Sunday of the Passion, Christians enter into Holy
Week. This day opens before the Christian community the

final period of preparation before the celebration of the Three Days, the Paschal Triduum of the Lord's passion, death, and resurrection.

In many churches, palm branches will be given to worshipers for the procession into the worship space. Following an ancient custom, many Christians bring their palms home and place them in the household prayer center, behind a cross or sacred image, or above the indoor lintel of the entryway.

At sunset on Maundy/Holy Thursday, Lent comes to an end as the church begins the celebration of the events through which Christ has become the life and the resurrection for all who believe.

Passion Sunday	Matt. 21:1-11	Ps. 118:1-2, 19-29
	Isa. 50:4-9a	Ps. 31:9-16
	Phil. 2:5-11	Matt. 26:14—27:66
M	John 12:1-11	
T	John 12:20-36	
W	John 13:21-32	

For prayer throughout the day
Into your hand I commit my spirit.   *Psalm 31:5*

A prayer for the last days of Lent
Almighty God,
you sent your Son, our Savior Jesus Christ,
to take our flesh upon him and to suffer death on the cross.
Grant that we may share his obedience to your will
and in the glorious victory of his resurrection;
through your Son, Jesus Christ our Lord,
who lives and reigns with you and the Holy Spirit,
one God, now and forever.
Amen.

THE THREE DAYS

The Paschal Triduum of the Lord's Passion, Death, and Resurrection

The Three Days are the pinnacle, the turning point, the culmination of the entire year. In the home and in the church community, special attention is given to these days through prayer and keeping greater silence until the great Vigil of Easter is celebrated. Many Christians keep a fast from food, work, and entertainment on Good Friday and Holy Saturday. In the home, preparations can be made for the celebration of Easter: cleaning, coloring eggs, baking Easter breads, gathering greens or flowers to adorn crosses and sacred images. In those communities where baptisms will be celebrated, prayers may be offered for those to be received into the church.

MAUNDY/HOLY THURSDAY

Hymn

Love consecrates the humblest act

Love consecrates the humblest act
  and haloes mercy's deeds;
it sheds a benediction sweet
  and hallows human needs.

When in the shadow of the cross
  Christ knelt and washed the feet
of his disciples, he gave us
  a sign of love complete.

Love serves and willing stoops to serve;
  what Christ in love so true
has freely done for one and all,
    let us now gladly do!
     Text: Silas B. McManus
     Tune: NEW BRITAIN (Amazing Grace)

Readings

Exod. 12:1-4, 11-14   Ps. 116:1-2, 12-19
1 Cor. 11:23-26   John 13:1-17, 31b-35

Prayers

Lord God,
in a wonderful sacrament
you have left us a memorial of your suffering and death.
May this sacrament of your body and blood so work in us
that the way we live

will proclaim the redemption you have brought;
for you live and reign with the Father and the Holy Spirit,
one God, now and forever.
Amen.

O Christ, write this commandment in our hearts:
"Love one another as I have loved you."

How holy is this feast in which Christ is our food:
his passion is recalled, grace fills our hearts,
and we receive a pledge of the glory to come.

Table prayer for the Three Days

We adore you, O Christ, and we bless you.
By your holy cross you have redeemed the world.
In peace, let us pray to the Lord.
Lord, have mercy.

Blessed are you, O Lord our God.
With this food strengthen us
on our journey from death to life.
We glory in the cross of Christ.
Raise us, with him,
to the joy of the resurrection,
through Christ our Lord.
Amen.

GOOD FRIDAY

Hymn

Sing, my tongue, the glorious battle

Sing, my tongue, the glorious battle;
   sing the ending of the fray.
Now above the cross, the trophy,
   sound the loud triumphant lay;
tell how Christ, the world's redeemer,
   as a victim won the day.

Faithful cross, true sign of triumph,
   be for all the noblest tree;
none in foliage, none in blossom,
   none in fruit your equal be;
symbol of the world's redemption,
   for your burden makes us free.

    Text: Venantius Honorius Fortunatus; tr. John Neale
    Tune: FORTUNATUS NEW or PICARDY (Let all mortal flesh keep
    silence)

Readings

Isa. 52:13—53:12   Ps. 22
Heb. 10:16-25   John 18:1—19:42

Prayers

Lord Jesus,
you carried our sins in your own body on the tree
so that we might have life.
May we and all who remember this day
find new life in you now and in the world to come,
where you live and reign with the Father and the Holy Spirit,
now and forever.
Amen.

We adore you, O Christ, and we bless you.
By your holy cross you have redeemed the world.

Jesus, remember me when you come into your kingdom.

HOLY SATURDAY/THE EASTER VIGIL

Hymn

At the Lamb's high feast

At the Lamb's high feast we sing
praise to our victorious king,
who has washed us in the tide
flowing from his pierced side.
   Alleluia!

Where the paschal blood is poured
death's dread angel sheathes the sword;
Israel's hosts triumphant go
through the wave that drowns the foe.
   Alleluia!

Praise we Christ, whose blood was shed,
paschal victim, paschal bread;
with sincerity and love
eat we manna from above.
   Alleluia!

Father, who the crown shall give,
Savior, by whose death we live,
Spirit, guide through all our days:
Three in One, your name we praise.
   Alleluia!

Text: Office hymn, 17th cent.; tr. Robert Campbell, alt.
Tune: SONNE DER GERECHTIGKEIT

Readings

Gen. 1:1—2:4a
Gen. 7:1—9:17
Gen. 22:1-18
Exod. 14:10-31; 15:20-21
Isa. 55:1-11
Prov. 8:1—9:6

Ezek. 36:24-28
Ezek. 37:1-14
Zeph. 3:14-20
Rom. 6:3-11
Ps. 114
Matt. 28:1-10

italics indicate optional readings

Prayers

At the lighting of the paschal candle:

May the light of Christ, rising in glory,
dispel the darkness of our hearts and minds.

The Easter Proclamation

This is indeed the paschal feast
in which the true Lamb is slain,
by whose blood the doorposts of the faithful are made holy.

This is the night in which, in ancient times,
you delivered our forebears, the children of Israel,
from the land of Egypt;
and led them, dry-shod, through the Red Sea.

This, indeed, is the night in which the darkness of sin
has been purged away by the rising brightness.
This is the night in which all who believe in Christ
are rescued from evil and the gloom of sin,
are renewed in grace, and are restored to holiness.

This is the night of which it is written:
"and the night is as clear as the day";
and, "then shall my night be turned into day."

Therefore, in this night of grace,
receive, O holy Father,
this evening sacrifice of praise.
  from the Exsultet

O God,
who made this most holy night
to shine with the glory of the Lord's resurrection:
Stir up in your church that spirit of adoption
which is given to us in baptism,
that we, being renewed both in body and mind,
may worship you in sincerity and truth;
through Jesus Christ our Lord,
who lives and reigns with you,
in the unity of the Holy Spirit,
one God, now and forever.
Amen.

O God,
you increase your church
by continuing to call all peoples to salvation.
Let the cleansing waters of baptism flow,
and by your love watch over those whom you have called;
through your Son, Jesus Christ our Lord.
Amen.

EASTER

If children are present in the home, they may be invited to create and/or place Easter symbols by a white candle or a bowl of water. These may include colored eggs, a small bouquet of garden flowers, a green plant, colored pictures of Easter animals (butterfly, deer, dolphin or other fish, lamb, peacock, pelican, phoenix, whale). If there is a cross or crucifix present in the home, it may be decorated with a garland of greens or flowers.

A hymn for Easter

Now all the vault of heaven resounds

Now all the vault of heav'n resounds
in praise of love that still abounds:
"Christ has triumphed! He is living!"
Sing, choirs of angels, loud and clear!
Repeat their song of glory here:
"Christ has triumphed! Christ has triumphed!"
Alleluia, alleluia, alleluia!

Oh, fill us, Lord, with dauntless love;
set heart and will on things above
that we conquer through your triumph;
grant grace sufficient for life's day
that by our lives we truly say:
Christ has triumphed! He is living!
Alleluia, alleluia, alleluia!

Adoring praises now we bring
and with the heav'nly blessed sing:
"Christ has triumphed! Alleluia!"
Be to the Father, and our Lord,
to Spirit blest, most holy God,
all the glory, never ending!
Alleluia, alleluia, alleluia!

> Text: Paul Z. Strodach
> Tune: LASST UNS ERFREUEN (All creatures of our God and King)

A psalm for Easter

Do not be afraid, he is not here;
for he has been raised, as he said.　　　*Matthew 28:5, 6*

There are glad songs of victory in the tents of the righteous:
"The right hand of the LORD does valiantly;
　　the right hand of the LORD is exalted;
　　the right hand of the LORD does valiantly."
I shall not die, but I shall live,
　　and recount the deeds of the LORD.
The LORD has punished me severely,
　　but he did not give me over to death.

Open to me the gates of righteousness,
　　that I may enter through them
　　and give thanks to the LORD.

This is the gate of the LORD;
　　the righteous shall enter through it.

I thank you that you have answered me
　　and have become my salvation.
The stone that the builders rejected
　　has become the chief cornerstone.

This is the LORD's doing;
   it is marvelous in our eyes.
This is the day that the LORD has made;
   let us rejoice and be glad in it.   *Psalm 118:15-24*

Readings for Easter

See the daily readings

A canticle for Easter

Worthy is Christ, the Lamb who was slain.
   See Revelation 5:12

Morning: The Song of Zechariah
Evening: The Song of Mary
Bedtime: The Song of Simeon

or

You are worthy, our Lord and God,
   to receive glory and honor and power,
for you created all things,
   and by your will they existed and were created.

You are worthy to take the scroll
   and to open its seals,
for you were slaughtered and by your blood you ransomed
      for God
   saints from every tribe and language and people and nation;
you have made them a kingdom and priests serving our God.

Worthy is the Lamb that was slaughtered
to receive power and wealth and wisdom and might
and honor and glory and blessing!

To the one seated on the throne and to the Lamb
be blessing and honor and glory and might
forever and ever!   *Revelation 4:11; 5:9-10, 12, 13*

A prayer for Easter

Risen Lord,
you appeared to your disciples
in the upper room, on a road, by the sea, and in a garden.
Enlighten us with your grace
so that we may welcome you among us
in the breaking of bread, in our daily labor,
in our travels, and in all signs of life restored.
You live and reign with the Father and the Holy Spirit,
one God, now and forever.
Amen.

Easter table prayer

Alleluia. Christ is risen!
  He is risen indeed. Alleluia!
This is the day that the Lord has made.
  Let us rejoice and be glad in it.

Blessed are you, O Lord our God.
Through the resurrection of Christ
you have brought us to the promised land.
We praise you for the gifts of this table
and for the feast of Easter joy.
Breathe your Spirit into us and all creation,
and renew the whole earth with your love.
We ask this through Christ our Lord.
Amen.

Other Easter texts

Christ has become our paschal sacrifice:
Let us feast with joy in the Lord. Alleluia.

Christians, to the paschal victim
   offer your thankful praises!
A Lamb the sheep redeeming: Christ, who only is sinless,
   reconciling sinners to the Father.
Death and life have contended
   in that combat stupendous;
the prince of life, who died, reigns immortal.

Speak, Mary, declaring,
   what you saw when wayfaring.
"The tomb of Christ, who is living,
   the glory of Jesus' resurrection;
bright angels attesting,
   the shroud and napkin resting.
My Lord, my hope, is arisen;
   to Galilee he goes before you."

Christ indeed from death is risen,
   our new life obtaining.
Have mercy, victor King, ever reigning!
   Amen.
    Victimae Paschali laudes; Wipo of Burgundy

O God,
you gave your only Son
to suffer death on the cross for our redemption,
and by his glorious resurrection
you delivered us from the power of death.
Make us die every day to sin,
so that we may live with him forever
in the joy of the resurrection;
through Jesus Christ our Lord,
who lives and reigns with you and the Holy Spirit,
one God, now and forever.
Amen.

DAILY READINGS AND PRAYERS

Resurrection of the Lord

S	Acts 10:34-43	Ps. 118:1-2, 14-24
	Col. 3:1-4	John 20:1-18
M	Exod. 14:10-31; 15:20-21	
T	Josh. 3:1-17	
W	Matt. 28:1-10	
Th	Song of Sol. 2:3-15	
F	Col. 3:1-17	
S	Exod. 15:1-18	

For prayer throughout the day
Do not be afraid: Christ has been raised from the dead.
See Matthew 28:5, 7

A prayer for the week
O God of life,
you have raised us with Christ
from the waters of baptism.
We have died and our lives are hidden with Christ in you.
Help us to live the baptism we have received with faith.
Amen.

Second Sunday of Easter

S	Acts 2:14a, 22-32	Ps. 16
	1 Peter 1:3-9	John 20:19-31
M	Jonah 1:1-17	
T	Jonah 2:1-10	
W	Matt. 12:38-42	

Th	1 Cor. 15:1-28
F	Ps. 88
S	Ps. 89:1-18

For prayer throughout the day
Without seeing you, O Christ, we love you.   *See 1 Peter 1:8*

A prayer for the week
O God, great is your mercy.
You have given us a new birth
through the resurrection of Christ
and an inheritance
that is imperishable, undefiled, and unfading.
O God, great is your mercy.
Amen.

Third Sunday of Easter

S	Acts 2:14a, 36-41	Ps. 116:1-4, 12-19
	1 Peter 1:17-23	Luke 24:13-35
M	Gen. 18:1-14	
T	Exod. 24:1-11	
W	John 21:1-14	
Th	Prov. 8:32—9:6	
F	1 Cor. 11:17-26	
S	Ps. 116	

For prayer throughout the day
Stay with us, risen Lord.   *See Luke 24:29*

A prayer for the week
Father in heaven,
we praise and thank you
that we have been born anew
through your living and faithful Word.
Amen.

Fourth Sunday of Easter

S	Acts 2:42-47	Ps. 23
	1 Peter 2:19-25	John 10:1-10
M	Ezek. 34:1-16	
T	Ezek. 34:17-31	
W	Matt. 20:17-28	
Th	Jer. 23:1-16	
F	Heb. 8:1-13	
S	Ps. 23	

For prayer throughout the day
The LORD is my shepherd, I shall not want. *Psalm 23:1*

A prayer for the week
Good Shepherd,
you call us by name to follow you.
Guide us with your word;
refresh us with the waters of life;
strengthen us with your bread and overflowing cup.
Amen.

Fifth Sunday of Easter

S	Acts 7:55-60	Ps. 31:1-5, 15-16
	1 Peter 2:2-10	John 14:1-14
M	Exod. 13:1-22	
T	Prov. 3:1-18	
W	John 8:31-59	
Th	Acts 6:8-15	
F	Acts 7:1-60	
S	Ps. 31	

For prayer throughout the day
You are the way, and the truth, and the life.   *See John 14:6*

A prayer for the week
Lord Jesus,
in the waters of baptism
you have made us a chosen race and a royal priesthood.
May we proclaim your gracious presence in word and deed.
Amen.

Sixth Sunday of Easter

S	Acts 17:22-31	Ps. 66:8-20
	1 Peter 3:13-22	John 14:15-21
M	Deut. 5:22-33	
T	Isa. 54:1-10	
W	Acts 17:32—18:11	

Ascension of the Lord	Acts 1:1-11	Ps. 47
	Eph. 1:15-23	Luke 24:44-53
F	Matt. 28:16-20	
S	Ps. 93	

For prayer throughout the day
Spirit of love, guide me this day.

A prayer for the week
Spirit of truth,
strengthen our hope,
help us to keep a clear conscience,
and give us peace in the face of adversity.
Amen.

Seventh Sunday of Easter

S	Acts 1:6-14	Ps. 68:1-10, 32-35
	1 Peter 4:12-14;	John 17:1-11
	5:6-11	
M	Lev. 9:1-24	
T	1 Kings 8:54-65	
W	John 3:31-36	
Th	Num. 16:41-50	
F	1 John 2:1-17	
S	Ps. 68:4-6, 24-35	

For prayer throughout the day
Spirit of God, restore us, support us, and strengthen us.

A prayer for the week
God our Creator,
through the presence of your Spirit
keep us steadfast in your Word
and strengthen our unity in Christ.
Amen.

Day of Pentecost

S	Acts 2:1-21	Ps. 104:24-34, 35b	
	1 Cor. 12:3b-13	John 20:19-23	
M	Joel 2:18-29		
T	Ezek. 39:7-9, 21-29		
W	Luke 1:26-38		
Th	Num. 11:24-30		
F	Gal. 5:13-26		
S	Ps. 104		

For prayer throughout the day
Come, Holy Spirit, and fill our hearts
with the fire of your love.

A prayer for the week
O God,
you have poured the Spirit of your Son
into our hearts at baptism.
May we listen to the Spirit who guides us to the truth
and teaches us the works of love.
Amen.

BLESSING OF THE HOUSEHOLD AT EASTER

The Gospels narrate the appearances of the risen Christ in many ordinary places: an apartment, a garden, on a roadside, at a sea-side breakfast. Over the centuries, Christians have grasped the significance of these stories by celebrating customs that welcome the risen Christ and ask God's blessing on household life. In many countries, certain foods and plants that speak of life springing up from death are central elements in such celebrations. They invite the members of the household to "taste" and "see" the resurrection: lamb, yeast breads, eggs, grains, spring garden flowers.

Whether you live alone or with others, you may invite friends and other family members to gather for this blessing. It may be used for a festive Easter Day meal, on one of the Sundays of Easter, or on any day when it is most appropriate for a particular household. One person may lead with the greeting and blessing while another may read the scripture reading.

Invitation

May the peace of the risen Christ
be with us and with all who enter this house.
Amen.

Come to him, a living stone, though rejected by mortals yet chosen and precious in God's sight, and like living stones, let yourselves be built into a spiritual house.   *1 Peter 2:4-5*

Reading

As we prepare to ask God's blessing on this household,
let us listen to the words of scripture.

As they came near the village to which they were going, *Jesus* walked ahead as if he were going on. But they urged him strongly, saying, "Stay with us, because it is almost evening and the day is now nearly over." So he went in to stay with them. When he was at the table with them, he took bread, blessed and broke it, and gave it to them. Then their eyes were opened, and they recognized him; and he vanished from their sight. They said to each other, "Were not our hearts burning within us while he was talking to us on the road, while he was opening the scriptures to us?"

Luke 24:28-32

Prayer of blessing

Let us pray.

God of power and might,
you raised Jesus from the darkness of death
and brought the light of salvation to all who believe.

As we celebrate his victory over death,
send your blessing upon us and all who enter this home.
Teach us to speak words of peace and hope.
Lead us to share our food with strangers and the hungry.
Inspire us to welcome every visitor as Christ himself.
We ask this through your Son, our Lord Jesus Christ,
who lives and reigns with you and the Holy Spirit,
one God, now and forever.
Amen.

The Lord's Prayer

Song

Christ is alive

Christ is alive! Let Christians sing.
The cross stands empty to the sky.
Let streets and homes with praises ring.
Love, drowned in death, shall never die.

Christ is alive! No longer bound
to distant years in Palestine,
but saving, healing, here and now,
and touching every place and time.

Christ is alive, and comes to bring
good news to this and every age,
'till earth and sky and ocean ring
with joy, with justice, love and praise.
 Text: Brian Wren
 Tune: TRURO or DUKE STREET (I know that my Redeemer lives)

THANKSGIVING FOR BAPTISM DURING EASTERTIME

During the Fifty Days of Easter, Christians celebrate the resurrection of Christ and their incorporation into his death and resurrection through Holy Baptism. While it is always appropriate to remember and offer thanksgiving on the anniversary of a baptism, the household may celebrate this thanksgiving for baptism during the Easter season.

When used, this thanksgiving may take place around a white baptismal/Easter candle set next to a bowl of water. If two or more persons are present, one may lead with the invitation and the prayer of blessing while the reading may be read by another person.

Many baptismal services include these or similar questions: *Do you intend to continue in the covenant God made with you in Holy Baptism: to live among God's faithful people, to hear his Word and share in his supper, to proclaim the good news of God in Christ through word and deed, to serve all people—following the example of our Lord Jesus, and to strive for justice and peace in all the earth?* After the Affirmation of Faith or after the Conclusion, those who celebrate this thanksgiving may discuss the practical ways in which they respond to these questions.

Invitation

Jesus Christ is the light of the world.
The light no darkness can overcome.

or

Let your light so shine before others
that they may see your good works
and glorify your Father in heaven.

Song

Baptized in water

Baptized in water, sealed by the Spirit,
   cleansed by the blood of Christ our King:
Heirs of salvation, trusting his promise,
   faithfully now God's praise we sing.

Baptized in water, sealed by the Spirit,
   dead in the tomb with Christ our King:
One with his rising, freed and forgiven,
   thankfully now God's praise we sing.

Baptized in water, sealed by the Spirit,
   marked with the sign of Christ our King:
Born of one Father, we are his children,
   joyfully now God's praise we sing.
     Text: Michael Saward
     Tune: BUNESSAN (Morning has broken)

Reading

Do you not know that all of us who have been baptized into
Christ Jesus were baptized into his death? Therefore we have
been buried with him by baptism into death, so that just as
Christ was raised from the dead by the glory of the Father,
so we too might walk in newness of life.   *Romans 6:3-4*

or

Like newborn infants, long for the pure, spiritual milk, so that by it you may grow into salvation—if indeed you have tasted that the Lord is good.   *1 Peter 2:2-3*

Affirmation of faith

All present may affirm their faith by professing the church's ancient baptismal creed.

I believe in God, the Father almighty,
　　creator of heaven and earth.

I believe in Jesus Christ, God's only Son, our Lord,
　　who was conceived by the Holy Spirit,
　　born of the Virgin Mary,
　　suffered under Pontius Pilate,
　　was crucified, died, and was buried;
　　he descended to the dead.
　　On the third day he rose again;
　　he ascended into heaven,
　　he is seated at the right hand of the Father,
　　and he will come to judge the living and the dead.

I believe in the Holy Spirit,
　　the holy catholic Church,
　　the communion of saints,
　　the forgiveness of sins,
　　the resurrection of the body,
　　and the life everlasting. Amen.

Prayer of thanksgiving

Let us pray.

Gracious God,
we thank you for the new life
you have given us in baptism:
for the holy cross traced on our foreheads;
for the waters of new birth;
for the saving Word that claimed us as your children;
for the light of Christ that shines in our midst.

Through the power of your Spirit,
bless us and strengthen us in the household of faith
so that we may continue to serve you and each other
in peace and love.
May the risen Christ be with us always
and lead us into the presence of your unfading light.
We ask this through your Son, our Lord Jesus Christ,
who lives and reigns with you and the Holy Spirit,
one God, now and forever.
Amen.

*Each person may dip a hand into the water and make the
sign of the cross in remembrance of his or her baptism.*

Prayers for others and ourselves

The Lord's Prayer

Conclusion

May the risen Christ bring us light and life
in these days of Easter rejoicing.
Amen. Alleluia.

PENTECOST

From ashes of Ash Wednesday to the fire and wind of Pentecost, Christians keep the Forty Days of Lent, the Three Days of the paschal feast, and the Fifty Days of Easter. On Pentecost Christians celebrate the coming of the Holy Spirit: the wind, the breath, the flame, the fire of Christ's presence throughout the world and within each believer. Pentecost has also been called "the festival of firstfruits," the first of the crop to ripen in the sun. Scripture calls Jesus "the firstfruit of the resurrection," raised by the powerful breathing, the life-giving light of God.

Christians pray to God "in the power of the Spirit." The gifts of the Spirit are faith, hope, and love. Whenever two or more gather in Jesus' name, the Spirit is present. At every baptism and eucharist, we pray for the Spirit's presence to forgive and strengthen, inspire and refresh. In the household, we pray for the Spirit's guidance, for the deepening of faith, hope, and love, for the patience and wisdom to live in peace with each other and our neighbors.

On the Saturday before Pentecost Sunday, it is the custom in many places to decorate the home with bright flowers (roses, peonies, poppies, and irises) and to gather at church for a great vigil service (similar to the Christmas Eve and Easter Eve vigils). If you cannot gather at church, household prayer may be celebrated using the following readings and texts.

Invitation

Let us praise God for the life-giving Spirit.
Come, Holy Spirit, inflame our waiting hearts.

Hymn

Come, Holy Ghost, our souls inspire

Come, Holy Ghost, our souls inspire,
and lighten with celestial fire;
thou the anointing Spirit art,
who dost thy sev'nfold gifts impart.

Thy blessed unction from above
is comfort, life, and fire of love.
Enable with perpetual light
the dullness of our blinded sight.

Anoint and cheer our soiled face
with the abundance of thy grace.
Keep far our foes; give peace at home;
where thou art guide, no ill can come.

Teach us to know the Father, Son,
and thee, of both, to be but one;
that through the ages all along
thy praise may be our endless song!

> Text: attr. Rhabanus Maurus; tr. John Cosin
> Tune: KOMM, GOTT SCHÖPFER or ERHALT UNS, HERR (Lord,
> keep us steadfast in your Word)

Readings

Acts 2:1-11   Ps. 33:12-22
Rom. 8:14-17, 22-27   John 7:37-39a

Prayers

Come, Holy Spirit, come,
and fill the hearts of your people.

Ven, Señor, Espíritu Creador,
a renovar la faz de la tierra.

Lord God,
you taught the hearts of your faithful people
by sending them the light of your Holy Spirit.
Grant that we, by your Spirit,
may have a right judgment in all things
and evermore rejoice in the Spirit's holy counsel;
through your Son, Jesus Christ our Lord.
Amen.

Almighty and ever-living God,
you fulfilled the promise of Easter
by sending your Holy Spirit
to unite the races and nations on earth
and thus to proclaim your glory.
Look upon your people gathered in prayer,
open to receive the Spirit's flame.
May the Spirit come to rest in our hearts
and heal the divisions of word and tongue,
that with one voice and one song
we may praise your name in joy and thanksgiving.
We ask this through your Son, Jesus Christ our Lord,
who lives and reigns with you and the Holy Spirit,
one God, now and forever.
Amen.

SUMMER • AUTUMN • NOVEMBER

From Advent to Pentecost, Christians celebrate the significant events in the life of Christ, from his nativity to his resurrection and sending of the Holy Spirit. The yearly focus on these events is not intended, however, to serve as a return—again and again—to the distant past. Rather, Christians ask God in prayer to continue those events in the present: to bring the Word to birth in human hearts (Advent/Christmas), to strengthen Christian witness among the nations (Epiphany), to help us return to God's mercy and forgiveness (Lent), to save women, children, and men through the waters of Christ's death and resurrection (Holy Week), to send the baptized forth from the font and the holy supper to proclaim good news (Easter), to guide Christians throughout daily life (Pentecost).

The weeks and months following the Day of Pentecost coincide with the natural seasons of summer, autumn, and late autumn/November. Christian communities refer to this time in different ways: the Pentecost season, Ordinary Time, or the Time of the Church. Whatever term is used to describe the many weeks between Pentecost and Christ the King (the last Sunday of the year), the seasons and calendars of North America offer some distinctive periods through which we may shape prayer in the household.

The Day of Pentecost is celebrated close to the end of the school year. Here an obvious connection exists between graduations/new beginnings and our prayer for the Spirit's guidance in new endeavors. School commencements tend to coincide with the beginning of summer (Memorial Day) while school openings usually take place around the beginning of September (Labor Day). For many people, the intervening months signal a slightly altered schedule attuned to the weather, harvests, and vacations. Summer months offer their unique grace to those who spend the time in discerning the many images which link the Scriptures and the patient growth of the seed in the soil.

The days of early autumn (September and October) herald the resumption of a more regular schedule: school begins, church education programs commence, and the steady rhythms of work are accompanied by cooling breezes and the changing colors of the landscape. In many church schools throughout the world, prayers are offered to Christ the Teacher, asking his guidance as students return to class. During these months, various crops—nuts, wine, and apples—are harvested and appear on roadside stands and in grocery stores. In many countries the harvest days of September and October are marked with prayer, feasting, and special care for the poor and hungry.

The month of November is unique in that it begins with All Saints Day (November 1) and ends with the feast of Christ the King/Reign of Christ (usually the last Sunday of November). The Sunday and daily readings seem to extend the harvest, but in a new way: They speak of God's harvest of *human beings* into their heavenly home. In the baptismal creed, Christians confess their belief in the communion of saints, the resurrection of the body, and life everlasting. November reveals—in many parts of the land—the death of summer's flourishing growth. It is a simple sign of human mortality, a reminder of death's presence. Perhaps, then, it is no coincidence that November's scriptural emphasis on the consummation of all things in Christ is reflected in the landscape and the chilling temperatures. Yet in the midst of this turning of the seasons and the reminders of death's presence, Christians hold forth the central feast of the year: the death and resurrection of Christ present in baptism and the holy supper. In these last days of the church's year, Christians are invited to celebrate the reign of Christ, whose death on the cross has transformed our deaths into the gate of everlasting life.

SUMMER

A song for summer

For the beauty of the earth
For the beauty of the earth, for the beauty of the skies,
for the love which from our birth over and around us lies:
Refrain: Christ, our Lord, to you we raise
this our sacrifice of praise.

For the joy of ear and eye, for the heart and mind's delight,
for the mystic harmony linking sense to sound and sight:
Refrain

For the joy of human love, brother, sister, parent, child,
friends on earth and friends above;
for all gentle thoughts and mild: *Refrain*

For yourself, best gift divine to the world so freely giv'n;
agent of God's grand design, peace on earth and joy in heav'n:
Refrain

Text: Folliott S. Pierpoint
Tune: DIX

A psalm for summer

In Christ all things in heaven and on earth were created,
things visible and invisible . . . all things have been created
through him and for him. *Colossians 1:16*

Bless the Lord, O my soul.
O Lord my God, you are very great.
You are clothed with honor and majesty,
wrapped in light as with a garment.

You stretch out the heavens like a tent,
  you set the beams of your chambers on the waters,
  the earth is satisfied with the fruit of your work.

You cause the grass to grow for the cattle,
  and plants for people to use,
to bring forth food from the earth,
  and wine to gladden the human heart,
oil to make the face shine,
  and bread to strengthen the human heart.

All *your creatures* look to you
  to give them their food in due season;
when you give to them, they gather it up;
  when you open your hand, they are filled with good things.
When you hide your face, they are dismayed;
  when you take away their breath, they die
  and return to their dust.
When you send forth your spirit, they are created;
  and you renew the face of the ground.
    Psalm 104:1-3, 13-15, 27-30

Readings for summer

See the daily readings

A canticle for summer

O LORD, how manifold are your works!
In wisdom you have made them all.   *Psalm 104:24*

Morning: The Song of Zechariah
Evening: The Song of Mary
Bedtime: The Song of Simeon

or

I. The Cosmic Order

O let the heavens bless the Lord.
Bless the Lord, you angels of the Lord;
   bless the Lord, all the heavenly hosts.

Praise and exalt our God forever.

Bless the Lord, you waters above the heavens;
   bless the Lord, sun and moon and stars of the sky.

Praise and exalt our God forever.

Bless the Lord, every shower of rain and fall of dew;
   bless the Lord, every breeze and gusty wind.

Praise and exalt our God forever.

Bless the Lord, fire and heat;
   bless the Lord, scorching wind and bitter cold.

Praise and exalt our God forever.

Bless the Lord, each drop of dew and flake of snow;
   bless the Lord, nights and days, light and darkness.

Praise and exalt our God forever.

Bless the Lord, frost and cold, ice and sleet;
   bless the Lord, thunderclouds and lightning flashes.

Praise and exalt our God forever.

II. The Earth and Its Creatures

O let the earth bless the Lord.
Bless the Lord, mountains and hills;
   bless the Lord, all that grows from the earth.

Praise and exalt our God forever.

Bless the Lord, O springs of water;
   bless the Lord, seas and rivers.

Praise and exalt our God forever.

Bless the Lord, you whales;
   bless the Lord, all that swim in the depths of the seas.

Praise and exalt our God forever.

Bless the Lord, all birds of the air;
   bless the Lord, beasts of the wild, flocks and herds.

Praise and exalt our God forever.

III. The People of God

O let all who dwell on the earth, bless the Lord.
Bless the Lord, men and women, children and youth;
   bless the Lord, all people everywhere.

Praise and exalt our God forever.

Bless the Lord, you people of God;
   bless the Lord, priests and all who serve the Lord.

Praise and exalt our God forever.

Bless the Lord, all who are upright in spirit;
   bless the Lord, all who are holy and humble in heart.

Praise and exalt our God forever.

The Song of the Three Young Men

Summer prayers

God of all light, life, and love,
through the visible things of this world
you raise our thoughts to things unseen,
and you show us your power and your love.
From your dwelling-place
refresh our hearts and renew the face of the earth
with the life-giving water of your Word,
until the new heaven and new earth
resound with the song of resurrection
in Jesus Christ our Lord.
Amen.

Almighty God,
we thank you for making the fruitful earth
produce what is needed for life.
Bless those who work in the fields;
give us favorable weather;
and grant that we may all share the fruits of the earth,
rejoicing in your goodness;
through your Son, Jesus Christ our Lord.
Amen.

O God, whose glory fills the whole creation,
and whose presence we find wherever we go:
Preserve *us/those* who travel:
surround *us/them* with your loving care;
protect *us/them* from every danger;
and bring *us/them* in safety to *our/their* journey's end;
through Jesus Christ our Lord.
Amen.

Summer table prayer

All you works of the Lord, bless the Lord.
Praise and magnify God forever.
All you green things that grow on the earth, bless the Lord.
Praise and magnify God forever.

O God of wonder,
the whole earth is full of your glory.
We give you thanks for the gifts of summer
and the blessings of this meal.
Teach us to share what we have received,
for you are the giver of all good things.
We ask this through Christ our Lord.
Amen.

DAILY READINGS AND PRAYERS

Trinity Sunday

S	Gen. 1:1—2:4a	Ps. 8
	2 Cor. 13:11-13	Matt. 28:16-20
M	Job 38:1-41	
T	Job 39:1—40:5	
W	John 14:15-25	
Th	1 Kings 8:1-30	
F	1 Cor. 12:1-13	
S	Ps. 29	

For prayer throughout the day
The Sacred Three be over me, the blessing of the Trinity.

A prayer for the week
May the grace of our Lord Jesus Christ, the love of God,
and the communion of the Holy Spirit be with us always.
Amen.

Sunday between May 29 and June 4 inclusive [Proper 4]

S	Deut. 11:18-21, 26-28	Ps. 31:1-5, 19-24
	Rom. 1:16-17; 3:22b-28	Matt. 7:21-29
M	Josh. 8:30-35	
T	Josh. 24:1-28	
W	Matt. 7:1-14	
Th	Job 28:1-28	
F	Rom. 2:1-11	
S	Ps. 31	

For prayer throughout the day
In you, O LORD, I seek refuge.   *Psalm 31:1*

A prayer for the week
Gracious God,
set our feet on the strong foundation of your Word
and strengthen our faith through your Spirit.
Amen.

Sunday between June 5 and June 11 inclusive [Proper 5]

S	Hosea 5:15—6:6	Ps. 50:7-15
	Rom. 4:13-25	Matt. 9:9-13, 18-26
M	Hosea 10:1-2, 9-10	
T	Hosea 14:1-9	
W	Matt. 12:1-8	
Th	Lev. 15:25-31; 22:1-9	
F	Heb. 13:1-16	
S	Ps. 50	

For prayer throughout the day
O God, deliver me in the day of trouble.   *See Psalm 50:15*

A prayer for the week
O God,
we trust your promise and cling to your Word.
Help us in our weakness.
Amen.

Sunday between June 12 and June 18 inclusive [Proper 6]

S	Exod. 19:2-8a	Ps. 100
	Rom. 5:1-8	Matt. 9:35—10:8
M	Josh. 1:1-18	
T	1 Sam. 3:1-10	
W	Luke 6:12-19	
Th	Prov. 4:10-27	
F	2 Thess. 2:13—3:5	
S	Ps. 105	

For prayer throughout the day
In you, Lord Jesus, the reign of heaven has come near.
See Matthew 10:7

A prayer for the week
Lord our God,
we give you thanks
for your love has been poured into our hearts
through the Holy Spirit.
Amen.

Sunday between June 19 and June 25 inclusive [Proper 7]

S	Jer. 20:7-13	Ps. 69:7-10, 16-18
	Rom. 6:1b-11	Matt. 10:24-39
M	Jer. 26:1-12	
T	Jer. 38:1-13	
W	Matt. 10:5-23	
Th	Jer. 26:20-24	
F	Rev. 2:1-11	
S	Ps. 69	

For prayer throughout the day
Let us walk with Christ.   *See Romans 6:4*

A prayer for the week
Lord Jesus,
give us courage
so that we may never hesitate
to speak your truth in the light of day.
Amen.

Sunday between June 26 and July 2 inclusive [Proper 8]

S	Jer. 28:5-9	Ps. 89:1-4, 15-18
	Rom. 6:12-23	Matt. 10:40-42
M	Jer. 18:1-11	
T	Jer. 30:1-11	
W	Mark 9:38-50	
Th	1 Kings 21:1-29	
F	1 John 4:1-6	
S	Ps. 119:153-168	

For prayer throughout the day
I will sing of your steadfast love, O LORD, forever.
Psalm 89:1

A prayer for the week
Lord Jesus,
may you always find our hearts
eager to welcome your gracious word.
Amen.

Sunday between July 3 and July 9 inclusive [Proper 9]

S	Zech. 9:9-12	Ps. 145:8-14
	Rom. 7:15-25a	Matt. 11:16-19, 25-30

M	Jer. 27:1-22
T	Jer. 28:1-17
W	John 13:1-11
Th	Lam. 5:1-22
F	Rom. 7:1-20
S	Ps. 145

For prayer throughout the day
Come to me, says the Lord, I will give you rest.
See Matthew 11:28

A prayer for the week
Most gracious God,
when I do not understand my actions,
when I do the very thing I hate,
forgive me and guide me to do
what is pleasing in your sight.
Amen.

Sunday between July 10 and July 16 inclusive [Proper 10]

S	Isa. 55:10-13	Ps. 65:9-13
	Rom. 8:1-11	Matt. 13:1-9, 18-23
M	Lev. 26:3-20	
T	Deut. 28:1-24	
W	Matt. 13:10-17	
Th	Prov. 11:23-30	
F	Eph. 4:17—5:2	
S	Ps. 65	

For prayer throughout the day
Spirit of God, lead me on the path of peace.

A prayer for the week
God the sower,
may the good seed of your Word
grow within our hearts.
May we understand it and put it into action.
Amen.

Sunday between July 17 and July 23 inclusive [Proper 11]

S	Isa. 44:6-8	Ps. 86:11-17
	Rom. 8:12-25	Matt. 13:24-30, 36-43
M	Nahum 1:1-13	
T	Zeph. 3:1-13	
W	Rev. 14:12-20	
Th	Dan. 12:1-13	
F	Gal. 4:21—5:1	
S	Ps. 86	

For prayer throughout the day
Abba! Father!   *Romans 8:15*

A prayer for the week
Teach me your way, O Lord,
that I may walk in your truth.
Give me an undivided heart.
Amen.

Sunday between July 24 and July 30 inclusive [Proper 12]

S	1 Kings 3:5-12	Ps. 119:129-136
	Rom. 8:26-39	Matt. 13:31-33, 44-52
M	1 Kings 3:15-28	

T	Prov. 1:1-33
W	Mark 4:30-34
Th	Lev. 2:1-11
F	Eph. 6:10-20
S	Ps. 119:121-128

For prayer throughout the day
If God is for us, who is against us?   *Romans 8:31*

A prayer for the week
O God,
send us your Spirit;
help us in our weakness;
deepen our love for you,
give us strength to heed your call.
Amen.

Sunday between July 31 and August 6 inclusive [Proper 13]

S	Isa. 55:1-5	Ps. 145:8-9, 14-21
	Rom. 9:1-5	Matt. 14:13-21
M	Deut. 8:1-10	
T	Deut. 26:1-11	
W	Matt. 15:32-39	
Th	Exod. 16:1-35	
F	Acts 2:37-47	
S	Ps. 78:1-29	

For prayer throughout the day
O LORD, you are near to those who call upon you.
    See Psalm 145:18

A prayer for the week
O God,
you open your hand
and satisfy the desire of every living thing.
You feed us with finest wheat.
For these good gifts we give you thanks.
Amen.

Sunday between August 7 and August 13 inclusive [Proper 14]

S	1 Kings 19:9-18	Ps. 85:8-13
	Rom. 10:5-15	Matt. 14:22-33
M	Gen. 7:11-24, 8:20—9:7	
T	Gen. 19:15-29	
W	John 6:15-21	
Th	Ps. 18:1-19	
F	Rom. 9:6—10:4	
S	Ps 85	

For prayer throughout the day
O Lord, I thank you for your steadfast love.
See Psalm 85:10

A prayer for the week
Lord, be with us when we are fearful.
Grant us the courage to follow your call
despite wind and waves.
May we walk steadily toward you all the days of our lives.
Amen.

Sunday between August 14 and August 20 inclusive [Proper 15]

S	Isa. 56:1, 6-8	Ps. 67
	Rom. 11:1-2a, 29-32	Matt. 15:21-28
M	2 Kings 5:1-27	
T	Isa. 60:8-16	
W	Matt. 15:1-20	
Th	Acts 15:1-35	
F	Rom. 11:1-36	
S	Ps. 87	

For prayer throughout the day
Have mercy on me, Lord.   *Matthew 15:22*

A prayer for the week
O God,
be gracious and bless us
and let your face shine upon us,
so that your ways may be known upon the earth
and your saving help among all nations.
Amen.

Sunday between August 21 and August 27 inclusive [Proper 16]

S	Isa. 51:1-6	Ps. 138
	Rom. 12:1-8	Matt. 16:13-20
M	Mal. 2:17—3:4	
T	Mal. 3:14—4:6	
W	Matt. 26:6-13	
Th	Deut. 32:9-39	
F	Gal. 1:18—2:21	
S	Ps. 18:1-3, 20-32	

For prayer throughout the day
You are the Messiah, the Son of the living God.
Matthew 16:16

A prayer for the week
O God,
give us wisdom
so that we may know your will
and discern what is good and acceptable.
Amen.

Sunday between August 28 and September 3 inclusive [Proper 17]

S	Jer. 15:15-21	Ps. 26:1-8
	Rom. 12:9-21	Matt. 16:21-28
M	2 Sam. 11:2-26	
T	2 Sam. 12:1-24	
W	Matt. 10:24-39	
Th	Jer. 17:5-18	
F	Rev. 3:1-13	
S	Ps. 26	

For prayer throughout the day
I keep the LORD always before me.   *Psalm 16:8*

A prayer for the week
Merciful God,
grant us grace to be patient in suffering
and steadfast in prayer,
to live in harmony with one another
and to serve you in everything.
Amen.

AUTUMN

A hymn for autumn

Sing to the Lord of harvest

Sing to the Lord of harvest, sing songs of love and praise;
with joyful hearts and voices your alleluias raise.
By him the rolling seasons in fruitful order move;
sing to the Lord of harvest a joyous song of love.

God makes the clouds drop fatness,
    the deserts bloom and spring,
the hills leap up in gladness, the valleys laugh and sing.
God fills them with his fullness, all things with large increase;
he crowns the year with goodness, with plenty and with peace.

Bring to this sacred altar the gifts his goodness gave,
the golden sheaves of harvest, the souls Christ died to save.
Your hearts lay down before him when at his feet you fall,
and with your lives adore him who gave his life for all.
    Text: John S. B. Monsell
    Tune: WIE LIEBLICH IST DER MAIEN
    or AURELIA (The Church's one foundation)

A psalm for autumn

God is able to provide you
with every blessing in abundance.   *2 Corinthians 9:8*

Hallelujah!
How good it is to sing praises to our God!
    how pleasant it is to honor the LORD with praise!

The LORD rebuilds Jerusalem
    and gathers the exiles of Israel.

The LORD heals the brokenhearted
    and binds up their wounds.

The LORD counts the number of the stars
    and calls them all by their names.

Great is our LORD and mighty in power,
    whose wisdom is beyond limit.

The LORD lifts up the lowly,
    but casts the wicked to the ground.

Sing to the LORD with thanksgiving;
    make music to our God upon the harp.

God covers the heavens with clouds
    and prepares rain for the earth;

God makes grass to grow upon the mountains
    and green plants to serve humankind.

God provides food for flocks and herds
    and for the young ravens when they cry.

The LORD is not impressed by the might of a horse
    and has no pleasure in the strength of a man;

But the LORD has pleasure in the God-fearing,
    in those who await God's gracious favor.
        Psalm 147:1-12

Readings for autumn

See the daily readings

A canticle for autumn

If you continue in my word, you are truly my disciples;
and you will know the truth,
and the truth will make you free.   John 8:31-32

Morning: The Song of Zechariah
Evening: The Song of Mary
Bedtime: The Song of Simeon

or

Happy are those who find wisdom,
  and those who get understanding,
for her income is better than silver,
  and her revenue better than gold.
She is more precious than jewels,
  and nothing you desire can compare with her.
Long life is in her right hand;
  in her left hand are riches and honor.
Her ways are ways of pleasantness,
  and all her paths are peace.
She is a tree of life to those who lay hold of her;
  those who hold her fast are called happy.

The Lord by wisdom founded the earth;
  by understanding he established the heavens;
by his knowledge the deeps broke open,
  and the clouds drop down the dew.
My child, do not let these escape from your sight:
  keep sound wisdom and prudence,
and they will be life for your soul
  and adornment for your neck.
Then you will walk on your way securely
  and your foot will not stumble.   *Proverbs 3:13-23*

Autumn prayers

Harvest

O gracious God,
when you open your hand
you satisfy the desire of every living thing.
Bless the land and waters,
and give the world a plentiful harvest;
let your Spirit go forth to renew the face of the earth.
As you show us your love and kindness
in the bounty of land and sea,
save us from selfish use of your gifts,
so that men and women everywhere may give you thanks;
through Jesus our Lord.
Amen.

Schools

O eternal God,
bless all schools, colleges, and universities,
that they may be lively places for sound learning,
new discovery, and the pursuit of wisdom;
and grant that those who teach and those who learn
may find you to be the source of all truth;
through Jesus Christ our Lord.
Amen.

Children

Almighty God,
you have blessed us with the joy and care of children.
As we bring them up,
give us calm strength and patient wisdom,
that we may teach them
to love whatever is just and true and good,
following the example of our Savior Jesus Christ.
Amen.

For the reform of the church

Gracious God,
we pray for your holy catholic church.
Fill it with all truth and peace.
Where it is corrupt, purify it;
where it is in error, direct it;
where in anything it is amiss, reform it;
where it is right, strengthen it;
where it is in need, provide for it;
where it is divided, reunite it;
for the sake of Jesus Christ, your Son our Savior.
Amen.

Autumn table prayer

The eyes of all wait upon you, O Lord,
   and you give them their food in due season.
You open wide your hand,
   and satisfy the needs of every living creature.

We praise you and bless you, O God,
for autumn days,
and for the gifts of this table.
Grant us grace to share your goodness,
until all people are fed by the harvest of the earth.
We ask this through Christ our Lord.
Amen.

DAILY READINGS AND PRAYERS

Sunday between September 4 and September 10 inclusive [Proper 18]

S   Ezek. 33:7-11   Ps. 119:33-40
     Rom. 13:8-14   Matt. 18:15-20
M   Lev. 4:27-35
T   Deut. 17:2-13
W   Matt. 18:1-14
Th   Exod. 34:11-28
F   Rom. 13:1-7
S   Ps. 119:57-72

For prayer throughout the day
Love your neighbor as yourself.   *Romans 13:9*

A prayer for the week
Teach me, O Lord,
the way of your statutes,
and I shall keep it to the end.
Give me understanding,
and I shall keep your law;
I shall keep it with all my heart.
Amen.

Sunday between September 11 and September 17 inclusive [Proper 19]

S   Gen. 50:15-21   Ps. 103:8-13
     Rom. 14:1-12   Matt. 18:21-35
M   Gen. 37:12-36
T   Gen. 41:53—42:17
W   Matt. 6:7-15
Th   Gen. 45:1-20

F   Rom. 16:1-20
S   Ps. 103

For prayer throughout the day
The LORD is merciful and gracious.   *Psalm 103:8*

A prayer for the week
Merciful God,
show us your love
and grant us charity of heart
that we might refrain from passing judgment
on our brothers and sisters.
Amen.

Sunday between September 18 and September 24 [Proper 20]

S   Jonah 3:10—4:11   Ps. 145:1-8
     Phil. 1:21-30   Matt. 20:1-16
M   Gen. 27:1-45
T   Gen. 28:10-17
W   Matt. 19:23-30
Th   Isa. 41:1-13
F   Rom. 14:13—15:3
S   Ps. 146

For prayer throughout the day
Live your life in a manner worthy of the gospel.   *Phil. 1:27*

A prayer for the week
O God,
you are gracious and merciful,
slow to anger and abounding in love.
Strengthen me with your grace and mercy,
your patience and love.
Amen.

Sunday between September 25 and October 1 inclusive [Proper 21]

S   Ezek. 18:1-4, 25-32   Ps. 25:1-9
       Phil. 2:1-13   Matt. 21:23-32
M   Num. 14:1-19
T   Num. 21:4-9
W   Matt. 3:1-12
Th   Josh. 4:1-24
F   Phil. 1:3-18
S   Ps. 25

For prayer throughout the day
To you, O LORD, I lift up my soul.   *Psalm 25:1*

A prayer for the week
O God,
we thank you that your Son came among us
as a servant.
May we have his mind:
to serve all those in need.
Amen.

Sunday between October 2 and October 8 inclusive [Proper 22]

S   Isa. 5:1-7   Ps. 80:7-15
       Phil. 3:4b-14   Matt. 21:33-46
M   Ezek. 19:10-14
T   Isa. 27:1-6
W   Matt. 8:5-13
Th   Song of Sol. 8:5-14
F   1 Peter 2:4-10
S   Ps. 118

For prayer throughout the day
O God, let your face shine on us today.   *See Psalm 80:3*

A prayer for the week
Gracious God,
grant us strength in the days ahead
that our lives may proclaim
the resurrection of the Lord Jesus.
Amen.

Sunday between October 9 and October 15 inclusive [Proper 23]

S	Isa. 25:1-9	Ps. 23
	Phil. 4:1-9	Matt. 22:1-14
M	Exod. 39:7-20	
T	Amos 9:5-15	
W	John 6:1-15, 25-35	
Th	Song of Sol. 7:10—8:4	
F	Phil. 3:13—4:1	
S	Ps. 34	

For prayer throughout the day
May the peace of God guard our hearts and minds.

A prayer for the week
Lord Jesus,
we thank you that in bread and cup
you offer us a rich feast
and the promise of life in your merciful embrace.
Amen.

Sunday between October 16 and October 22 inclusive [Proper 24]

S	Isa. 45:1-7	Ps. 96:1-9
	1 Thess. 1:1-10	Matt. 22:15-22
M	Dan. 3:1-30	
T	Dan. 6:1-28	
W	Matt. 17:22-27	
Th	Isa. 45:9-25	
F	Phil. 4:10-23	
S	Ps. 96	

For prayer throughout the day
The LORD our God calls you by your name.　　*Isaiah 45:4*

A prayer for the week
O God,
strengthen us to speak and live
your word with conviction, grace, and joy.
Amen.

Sunday between October 23 and October 29 inclusive [Proper 25]

S	Lev. 19:1-2, 15-18	Ps. 1
	1 Thess. 2:1-8	Matt. 22:34-46
M	Deut. 6:1-9, 20-25	
T	Deut. 10:10-22	
W	Matt. 19:16-22	
Th	Prov. 16:1-20	
F	James 2:8-26	
S	Ps. 110	

For prayer throughout the day
O LORD, watch over us this day.　　*See Psalm 1:6*

A prayer for the week
Merciful God,
grant us the grace to love you
with heart, soul, and mind.
Grant us the grace to see Christ
in friend, neighbor, and stranger.
Amen.

In church communities where it is celebrated

Reformation Day, October 31 or the last Sunday in October

Jer. 31:31-34   Ps. 46
Rom. 3:19-28   John 8:31-36

NOVEMBER

A song for November

O God, our help in ages past

O God, our help in ages past,
   our hope for years to come,
our shelter from the stormy blast,
   and our eternal home:

Under the shadow of your throne
   your saints have dwelt secure;
sufficient is your arm alone,
   and our defense is sure.

Time, like an ever-rolling stream,
   soon bears us all away;
we fly forgotten, as a dream
   dies at the op'ning day.

O God, our help in ages past,
   our hope for years to come,
still be our guard while troubles last
   and our eternal home!
     Text: Isaac Watts
     Tune: ST. ANNE

A psalm for November

Come, you that are blessed by my Father,
inherit the kingdom prepared for you
from the foundation of the world.   *Matthew 25:34*

At all times I will bless the LORD,
   whose praise shall ever be in my mouth.

I will glory in the LORD;
   let the humble hear and rejoice.

Proclaim with me the greatness of the LORD;
   let us exalt the name of the LORD together.

I sought the LORD, who answered me
   and delivered me out of all my terror.

Look upon the LORD and be radiant,
   and let not your faces be ashamed.

I called in my affliction and the LORD heard me
   and saved me from all my troubles.

The angel of the LORD encompasses the God-fearing,
   and the LORD will deliver them.

Taste and see that the LORD is good;
   happy are they who trust in the LORD!

The eyes of the LORD are upon the righteous,
   and the ears of the LORD are open to their cry.

The face of the LORD is against those who do evil,
   to root out the remembrance of them from the earth.

The righteous cry, and the LORD hears them
   and delivers them from all their troubles.

The LORD is near to the brokenhearted
   and will save those whose spirits are crushed.

Many are the troubles of the righteous,
   but the LORD will deliver the just out of them all.

The LORD will keep safe the bones of the righteous;
   not one of them shall be broken.

Evil shall slay the wicked,
   and those who hate the righteous will be punished.

The LORD ransoms the life of those chosen to serve,
and none will be punished who trust in the LORD.
Psalm 34:1-8, 15-22

Readings for November

See the daily readings

A canticle for November

*The Lamb at the center of the throne will be their shepherd,
and he will guide them to springs of the water of life.*
Revelation 7:17

Morning: The Song of Zechariah
Evening: The Song of Mary
Bedtime: The Song of Simeon

or

Alleluia!
For our paschal lamb, Christ, has been sacrificed.
Therefore, let us celebrate the festival,
not with the old yeast, the yeast of malice and evil,
but with the unleavened bread of sincerity and truth.

Christ, being raised from the dead, will never die again;
death no longer has dominion over him.
The death he died, he died to sin, once for all;
but the life he lives, he lives to God.
So you also must consider yourselves dead to sin
and alive to God in Christ Jesus.

Christ has been raised from the dead,
the first fruits of those who have died.
For since death came through a human being,
the resurrection of the dead
has also come through a human being.

For as all die in Adam,
so will all be made alive in Christ.
Alleluia!
1 Corinthians 5:7-8; Romans 6:9-11; 1 Corinthians 15:20-22

Prayers for November

The saints

Almighty God,
whose people are knit together in one holy church,
the body of Christ our Lord:
Grant us grace to follow your blessed saints
in lives of faith and commitment,
and to know the inexpressible joys you have prepared
for those who love you;
through your Son, Jesus Christ our Lord,
who lives and reigns with you and the Holy Spirit,
one God, now and forever.
Amen.

We give thanks to you, O Lord our God,
for all your servants and witnesses of time past:
for Abraham and Sarah;
for Moses and Aaron;
for Miriam and Joshua,
Deborah and Gideon, Samuel and Hannah;
for Isaiah and all the prophets;
for Mary, the mother of our Lord;
for Peter and Paul and all the apostles;
for Mary, Martha, and Mary Magdalene;
for Stephen, the first martyr, and all the saints and martyrs
in every time and in every land.
In your mercy, give us, as you gave them,

the hope of salvation and the promise of eternal life;
through the first-born from the dead, Jesus Christ our Lord.
Amen.

The faithful departed

With reverence and affection we remember before you,
O everlasting God,
all our departed friends and relatives.
Keep us in union with them here
through faith and love toward you,
that hereafter we may enter into your presence
and be numbered with those who serve you
and look upon your face in glory everlasting,
through your Son, Jesus Christ our Lord.
Amen.

At a grave

Almighty God,
by the death and burial of Jesus, your anointed,
you have destroyed death
and sanctified the graves of all your saints.
Keep our beloved dead in the company of all your saints
and, at the last,
raise them up to share with all your faithful people
the endless joy and peace
won through the glorious resurrection of Christ our Lord,
who lives and reigns with you and the Holy Spirit,
one God, now and forever.
Amen.

A prayer for mercy

O Lord,
support us all the day long of this troubled life,
until the shadows lengthen

and the evening comes
and the busy world is hushed,
the fever of life is over,
and our work is done.
Then, Lord, in your mercy,
grant us a safe lodging, and a holy rest,
and peace at the last;
through Jesus Christ our Lord.
Amen.

Day of Thanksgiving

Almighty God,
your generous goodness comes to us new every day.
By the work of your Spirit
lead us to acknowledge your goodness,
give thanks for your benefits,
and serve you in willing obedience;
through your Son, Jesus Christ our Lord.
Amen.

November table prayer

The eternal God is our dwelling place.
Blessed is the Lord, our strength and our salvation.

Stay with us, God of life,
as we share the bounty of this food and drink.
We give you thanks
for those who have gone before us in faith.
Bring us, with them,
to the harvest of everlasting life,
where all people will feast forever at your abundant table.
We ask this through Christ our Lord.
Amen.

DAILY READINGS AND PRAYERS

Sunday between October 30 and November 5 inclusive [Proper 26]

S	Micah 3:5-12	Ps. 43
	1 Thess. 2:9-13	Matt. 23:1-12
M	Ezek. 12:1-28	
T	Ezek. 13:1-16	
W	Matt. 23:13-39	
Th	Mal. 1:6—2:10	
F	1 Thess. 2:14-20	
S	Ps. 119:129-144	

For prayer throughout the day
O God, send out your light and your truth.   *Psalm 43:3*

A prayer for the week
God of compassion,
when my soul is cast down
and my heart is filled with many concerns,
be my strength, my refuge, and my hope.
Amen.

All Saints, November 1 or the first Sunday in November

| Rev. 7:9-17 | Ps. 34:1-10, 22 |
| 1 John 3:1-3 | Matt. 5:1-12 |

Sunday between November 6 and November 12 inclusive [Proper 27]

S	Amos 5:18-24	Ps. 70
	1 Thess. 4:13-18	Matt. 25:1-13
M	Joel 1:1-20	
T	Joel 2:21-32	
W	Matt. 24:1-28	

Th   Amos 8:1-14
F   1 Thess. 3:6—4:12
S   Ps. 71

For prayer throughout the day
We will be with the Lord forever.   *1 Thessalonians 4:17*

A prayer for the week
Lord Jesus,
may we be alert and watchful,
always ready to welcome you this day.
Amen.

Sunday between November 13 and November 19 inclusive [Proper 28]

S   Zeph. 1:7, 12-18   Ps. 90:1-8, 12
      1 Thess. 5:1-11   Matt. 25:14-30
M   Zech. 1:7-17
T   Zech. 3:1-10
W   Matt. 24:29-51
Th   Job 16:1-17
F   1 Thess. 5:12-28
S   Ps. 90

For prayer throughout the day
Keep us, Lord, as children of light.   *See 1 Thessalonians 5:5*

A prayer for the week
Lord Jesus Christ,
clothe us in the garments of faith, hope, and love.
May we be prepared to meet you now
and at the hour of our death.
Amen.

Christ the King/Reign of Christ [Proper 29]

S	Ezek. 34:11-16, 20-24	Ps. 95:1-7a
	Eph. 1:15-23	Matt. 25:31-46
M	Ezek. 20:1-8a, 33-42	
T	Ezek. 33:7-20	
W	John 5:19-47	
Th	Ps. 7	
F	Rev. 19:1-9	
S	Ps. 95	

For prayer throughout the day
Lord Jesus, help me to see and to serve you in the needy.
See Matthew 25:37

A prayer for the week
O God,
enlighten us with your grace,
so that we may serve you
in the hungry, the thirsty,
the stranger, the naked,
the sick, and the prisoner.
Give us eyes that see and ears that listen.
Amen.

BLESSING OF THE HOUSEHOLD FOR THANKSGIVING DAY

Invitation at table

We gather this day to give thanks to God
for the gifts of this land and its people,
for God has been generous to us.
As we ask God's blessing upon this food we will share,
may we be mindful of the lonely and the hungry.

Reading

As we prepare to offer thanks to God,
let us listen to the words of scripture:

I give thanks to my God always for you because of the grace
of God that has been given you in Christ Jesus, for in every
way you have been enriched in him, in speech and knowledge
of every kind—just as the testimony of Christ has been
strengthened among you—so that you are not lacking in any
spiritual gift as you wait for the revealing of our Lord Jesus
Christ. He will also strengthen you to the end, so that you
may be blameless on the day of our Lord Jesus Christ.
  1 Corinthians 1:4-8

Prayer of blessing

Let us pray.

God most provident,
we join all creation in offering you praise through Jesus Christ.
For generations the people of this land
have sung of your bounty.
With them, we offer you thanksgiving

for the rich harvest we have received at your hands.
Bless us and this food that we share with grateful hearts.
Continue to make our land fruitful
and let our love for you be seen
in our pursuit of justice and peace
and in our generous response to those in need.
We ask this through Christ our Lord.
Amen.

May Christ, the living bread,
bring us to the feast of eternal life.
Amen.

VISITING A CEMETERY

The Sunday and daily readings of November invite us to contemplate the resurrection of the body and the life of the world to come. From the perspective of Christian faith, the living and the dead are bound together in the communion of saints. Though the dead rest from their labors, they are united with the living under the canopy of God's mercy.

While we may visit the final resting place of a relative or friend at any time of the year, it is especially appropriate during Eastertime and the month of November, when the festival days celebrate the consummation of all things in Christ.

It is the custom among some people to bring flowers or evergreen branches to the cemetery. Others make a garland of greens in the shape of a cross to place on the grave.

When making such a visit or when remembering the beloved dead at home, any or all parts of this order may be used.

Invitation

I am the resurrection and the life, says the Lord.
Those who believe in me, even though they die, will live,
and everyone who lives and believes in me will never die.

Psalm

If we have died with Christ, we will also live with him.
  2 Timothy 2:11

I lift up my eyes to the hills;
  from where is my help to come?

My help comes from the LORD,
  the maker of heaven and earth.

The LORD will not let your foot be moved,
  and the One who watches over you will not fall asleep.

Behold, the One who keeps watch over Israel
  shall neither slumber nor sleep;

It is the LORD who watches over you;
  the LORD is your shade at your right hand,

So that the sun shall not strike you by day,
  nor the moon by night.

The LORD shall preserve you from all evil;
  the LORD shall keep you safe.

The LORD shall watch over your going out and your coming in,
  from this time forth for evermore.   *Psalm 121*

Reading

Christ has been raised from the dead, the first fruits of those
who have died. For since death came through a human being,
the resurrection of the dead has also come through a human
being; for as all die in Adam, so all will be made alive in
Christ. But each in his own order: Christ the first fruits, then
at his coming those who belong to Christ. Then comes the
end, when he hands over the kingdom to God the Father,
after he has destroyed every ruler and every authority and
power. For he must reign until he has put all his enemies
under his feet. The last enemy to be destroyed is death.

Thanks be to God, who gives us the victory through our Lord
Jesus Christ.
  1 Corinthians 15:20-26, 57

Prayers

For the sick and dying

O God,
comfort with the grace of your Holy Spirit
all who are in sorrow or need, sickness or adversity.
Have mercy on those to whom death draws near.
Bring consolation to those in sorrow or mourning.
And to all grant your love, taking them into your tender care.
We ask this through Christ our Lord.
Amen.

In thanksgiving for the faithful departed

O God,
we remember with thanksgiving
those who have loved and served you on earth,
who now rest from their labors
[especially those most dear to us, . . .].
Keep us in union with all your saints,
and bring us at last to the joy of your heavenly kingdom;
through Jesus Christ our Lord.
Amen.

Rest eternal grant *him/her*, O Lord;
and let light perpetual shine upon *him/her*.

For a peaceful death

Lord Jesus,
by your death you took away the sting of death.
Strengthen us to follow in faith where you have led the way,
that we may at length fall asleep peacefully in you
and wake in your likeness;
to you, the author and giver of life,
be all honor and glory, now and forever.
Amen.

The Lord's Prayer

Song

An appropriate song may be sung, such as:

> *Amazing grace*
> *Children of the heav'nly Father*
> *I know that my Redeemer lives*
> *O God, our help in ages past*

CHURCH YEAR CALENDAR FOR YEAR OF MATTHEW (CYCLE A)

Festivals and Sundays	1995-96	1998-99	2001-02	2004-05	2007-08
First Sunday in Advent	Dec. 3	Nov. 29	Dec. 2	Nov. 28	Dec. 2
The Baptism of Our Lord *First Sunday after the Epiphany*	Jan. 7	Jan. 10	Jan. 13	Jan. 9	Jan. 13
The Transfiguration of Our Lord *Last Sunday after the Epiphany*	Feb. 18	Feb. 14	Feb. 10	Feb. 6	Feb. 3
Ash Wednesday	Feb. 21	Feb. 17	Feb. 13	Feb. 9	Feb. 6
First Sunday in Lent	Feb. 25	Feb. 21	Feb. 17	Feb. 13	Feb. 10
Sunday of the Passion *Palm Sunday*	Mar. 31	Mar. 28	Mar. 24	Mar. 20	Mar. 16
Maundy Thursday Good Friday The Resurrection of Our Lord *Vigil of Easter* *Easter Day*	Apr. 4 Apr. 5 Apr. 6 Apr. 7	Apr. 1 Apr. 2 Apr. 3 Apr. 4	Mar. 28 Mar. 29 Mar. 30 Mar. 31	Mar. 24 Mar. 25 Mar. 26 Mar. 27	Mar. 20 Mar. 21 Mar. 22 Mar. 23
The Ascension of Our Lord	May 16	May 13	May 9	May 5	May 1
The Day of Pentecost	May 26	May 23	May 19	May 15	May 11
The Holy Trinity *First Sunday after Pentecost*	June 2	May 30	May 26	May 22	May 18
Sixth Sunday after Pentecost	July 7	July 4	June 30	June 26	June 22
Tenth Sunday after Pentecost	Aug. 4	Aug. 1	July 28	July 24	July 20
Fourteenth Sunday a. Pentecost	Sept. 1	Aug. 29	Aug. 25	Aug. 21	Aug. 17
Nineteenth Sunday a. Pentecost	Oct. 6	Oct. 3	Sept. 29	Sept. 25	Sept. 21
Day of Thanksgiving—Canada	Oct. 14	Oct. 11	Oct. 14	Oct. 10	Oct. 13
Twenty-third Sunday a. Pentecost	Nov. 3	Oct. 31	Oct. 27	Oct. 23	Oct. 19
Christ the King *Last Sunday after Pentecost*	Nov. 24	Nov. 21	Nov. 24	Nov. 20	Nov. 23
Day of Thanksgiving—U.S.A.	Nov. 28	Nov. 25	Nov. 28	Nov. 24	Nov. 27

ACKNOWLEDGMENTS

Unless otherwise noted below, songs, prayers, and blessings that are published in this collection are copyrighted by Augsburg Fortress.

Except for those psalms noted in the Acknowledgments section, scripture quotations are from the New Revised Standard Version Bible, copyright © 1989 Division of Christian Education of the National Council of the Churches of Christ in the United States of America. Used by permission.

DAILY PRAYER

Psalm 139:7-9: *The Book of Common Prayer* psalter (1979 edition).

Our Father in heaven: The English translation of the Lord's Prayer prepared by the English Language Liturgical Consultation (ELLC), 1988.

Gloria Patri: The English translation of the Gloria Patri prepared by the English Language Liturgical Consultation (ELLC), 1988.

UPON WAKING

I arise today (Saint Patrick's Breastplate): Public domain.

Glory to God in the highest: The English translation of the Gloria in Excelsis prepared by the English Language Liturgical Consultation (ELLC), 1988.

Holy, Holy, Holy: The English translation of the Sanctus prepared by the English Language Liturgical Consultation (ELLC), 1988.

I give thanks to you, my heavenly Father: *A Contemporary Translation of Luther's Small Catechism,* trans. Timothy J. Wengert, copyright © 1994 Augsburg Fortress.

MORNING PRAYER

O Splendor of the Father's light: Text copyright © 1978 *Lutheran Book of Worship.*

Psalm 95:1-7: *Psalter for the Christian People,* copyright © 1993 The Liturgical Press. Reprinted by permission.

Blessed are you, Lord, the God of Israel (Song of Zechariah): The English translation of the Benedictus prepared by the English Language Liturgical Consultation (ELLC), 1988.

Psalm 121: *Psalter for the Christian People,* copyright © 1993 The Liturgical Press. Reprinted by permission.

AT NOON

Blessed Savior, at this hour you hung upon the cross: Collect from Noonday Prayer, *The Book of Common Prayer* (1979 edition).

EVENING PRAYER

Jesus, joyous light of glory: Text copyright © 1994 Stephen P. Starke. Reprinted by permission.

Psalm 141:2: *The Book of Common Prayer* psalter (1979 edition).

My soul proclaims the greatness of the Lord (Magnificat): The English translation of the Magnificat prepared by the English Language Liturgical Consultation (ELLC), 1988.

Keep watch, dear Lord: Collect from Daily Evening Prayer: Rite One, *The Book of Common Prayer* (1979 edition).

AT BEDTIME

Now, Lord, you let your servant go in peace (Nunc dimittis): The English translation of the Nunc Dimittis prepared by the English Language Liturgical Consultation (ELLC), 1988.

I give thanks to you, my heavenly Father: *A Contemporary Translation of Luther's Small Catechism,* trans. Timothy J. Wengert, copyright © 1994 Augsburg Fortress.

Visit this house: Collect from Compline, *The Book of Common Prayer* (1979 edition).

Night prayers with children: Public domain.

Go, my children, with my blessing: Text copyright © 1983 Jaroslav J. Vajda. Reprinted by permission.

All praise to thee, my God: Text, public domain.

O Christ, you are the light (tr. Copeland): Text, public domain.

Children of the heavenly Father: Text copyright © 1978 *Lutheran Book of Worship.*

All through the night: Text, public domain.

SUNDAY

O radiant Light, O Sun divine (Phos Hilaron): Trans. copyright © William G. Storey. Reprinted by permission.

Psalm 118:1-4, 14-17: *Psalter for the Christian People,* copyright © 1993 The Liturgical Press. Reprinted by permission.

Thanksgiving for baptism: Adapted from *Lutheran Book of Worship* (p. 122), copyright © 1978.

We praise you, O God (Te Deum): The English translation of the Te Deum Laudamus prepared by the English Language Liturgical Consultation (ELLC), 1988.

O God, for our redemption: *Lutheran Book of Worship* (p. 20), copyright © 1978.

Psalm 34:8: *Psalter for the Christian People,* copyright © 1993 The Liturgical Press. Reprinted by permission.

Blessed are you, O Lord our God, who give nourishment to all your creatures: *Springtime of the Liturgy,* copyright © 1979 The Liturgical Press. Reprinted by permission.

We thank you, our Father: *Springtime of the Liturgy,* copyright © 1979 The Liturgical Press. Reprinted by permission.

O Christ, you are the light (tr. Quinn): *Hymnal for the Hours,* trans. copyright © 1989 GIA Publications, Inc. Reprinted by permission.

Psalm 110:1-5, 7: *Psalter for the Christian People,* copyright © 1993 The Liturgical Press. Reprinted by permission.

Lord God, whose Son our Savior Jesus Christ: Collect from Daily Evening Prayer: Rite Two, *The Book of Common Prayer* (1979 edition).

ADVENT

The King shall come when morning dawns: Text, public domain.

God of all wisdom: Adapted from the opening prayer for the First Sunday in Advent, *The Roman Missal,* copyright © 1975 International Committee on English in the Liturgy.

The O-Antiphons: *Lutheran Book of Worship* (pp. 174-175), copyright © 1978.

O Savior, rend the heavens wide: Trans. copyright © 1969 Concordia Publishing House. Reprinted by permission.

Oh, come, oh, come, Emmanuel: Text, public domain.

CHRISTMAS

What child is this: Text, public domain.

Psalm 110:3: *The Book of Common Prayer* psalter (1979 edition).

Psalm 98: *Psalter for the Christian People,* copyright © 1993 The Liturgical Press. Reprinted by permission.

Glory to God in the highest: The English translation of the Gloria in Excelsis prepared by the English Language Liturgical Consultation (ELLC), 1988.

Almighty God, you wonderfully created: *Lutheran Book of Worship* (p. 14), copyright © 1978.

Oh, come, oh, come, Emmanuel: Text, public domain.

Away in a manger: Text, public domain.

Go tell it on the mountain: Text, public domain.

We three kings: Text, public domain.

Noche de paz: *El Pueblo de Dios Canta: Adviento, Navidad, Epifanía y otros,* trans. copyright © 1989 Augsburg Fortress.

Grant us grace, O Lord: *Lutheran Book of Worship* (p. 30), copyright © 1978.

Merciful Lord, let the brightness of your light shine on your church: *Lutheran Book of Worship* (p. 31), copyright © 1978.

We remember today, O God: *Lutheran Book of Worship* (p. 31), copyright © 1978.

Eternal Father, you have placed us in a world of space and time: *Lutheran Book of Worship* (p. 41), copyright © 1978.

Eternal Father, you gave your Son the name of Jesus: *Lutheran Book of Worship* (p. 31), copyright © 1978.

EPIPHANY

When Christ's appearing was made known: Text, public domain.

Lord God, on this day you revealed your Son to the nations: *Lutheran Book of Worship* (p. 15), copyright © 1978.

Father in heaven, at the baptism of Jesus: *Lutheran Book of Worship* (p. 15), copyright © 1978.

We pray that you bless this home: *Lutheran Book of Worship: Occasional Services* (p. 190), copyright © 1982.

As with gladness men of old: Text, public domain.

Almighty God, you inspired Simon Peter: *Lutheran Book of Worship* (p. 31), copyright © 1978.

God our Father, your Son Jesus prayed that his followers might be one: *Lutheran Book of Worship* (p. 39), copyright © 1978.

Lord God, through the preaching of your apostle Paul: *Lutheran Book of Worship* (p. 32), copyright © 1978.

LENT

Almighty and ever-living God, you hate nothing you have made: *Lutheran Book of Worship* (p. 17), copyright © 1978.

As the sun with longer journey: *Collegeville Hymnal,* text copyright © 1990 Order of Saint Benedict, Inc. Reprinted by permission of The Liturgical Press.

O Lord God, you led your ancient people: Adapted from *Lutheran Book of Worship* (p. 17), copyright © 1978.

THE THREE DAYS

Love consecrates the humblest act: Text, public domain.

Lord God, in a wonderful sacrament: *Lutheran Book of Worship* (p. 20), copyright © 1978.

Sing, my tongue, the glorious battle: Text, public domain.

Lord Jesus, you carried our sins: *Lutheran Book of Worship* (p. 20), copyright © 1978.

At the Lamb's high feast we sing: Text, public domain.

This is indeed the paschal feast (The Easter Proclamation): *Lutheran Book of Worship: Ministers Edition* (p. 146), copyright © 1978.

O God, who made this most holy night to shine: Collect from the Great Vigil of Easter, *The Book of Common Prayer* (1979 edition).

O God, you increase your church: *Lutheran Book of Worship: Ministers Edition* (p. 149), copyright © 1978.

EASTER

Now all the vault of heaven resounds: Text copyright © 1958 Service Book and Hymnal.

Christians, to the paschal victim (Victimae Paschali laudes): Text, public domain.

O God, you gave your only Son: *Lutheran Book of Worship* (p. 20), copyright © 1978.

Christ is alive: Text copyright © 1975, 1993 Hope Publishing Company, Carol Stream IL 60188. All rights reserved. Reprinted by permission.

Baptized in water: Text copyright © 1982 Hope Publishing Company, Carol Stream IL 60188. All rights reserved. Reprinted by permission.

I believe in God, the Father almighty (The Apostles' Creed): The English translation of the Apostles' Creed prepared by the English Language Liturgical Consultation (ELLC), 1988.

Come, Holy Ghost, our souls inspire: Text, public domain.

Lord God, you taught the hearts of your faithful people: *Lutheran Book of Worship* (p. 47), copyright © 1978.

Almighty and ever-living God, you fulfilled the promise of Easter: *Lutheran Book of Worship* (p. 23), copyright © 1978.

SUMMER

For the beauty of the earth: Text, public domain.

O let the heavens bless the Lord (Song of the Three Young Men): Public domain.

God of all light, life, and love: *Lutheran Book of Worship: Ministers Edition* (p. 410), copyright © 1978.

Almighty God, we thank you for making the fruitful earth: *Lutheran Book of Worship* (p. 45), copyright © 1978.

O God, whose glory fills the whole creation: Adapted from the prayer for travelers in Prayers and Thanksgivings, *The Book of Common Prayer* (1979 edition).

AUTUMN

Sing to the Lord of harvest: Text, public domain.

Psalm 147:1-12: *Psalter for the Christian People,* copyright © 1993 The Liturgical Press. Reprinted by permission.

O gracious God, when you open your hand: *Lutheran Book of Worship* (p. 49), copyright © 1978.

O eternal God, bless all schools, colleges, and universities: *Lutheran Book of Worship* (p. 44), copyright © 1978.

Almighty God, you have blessed us with the joy and care of children: *Lutheran Book of Worship* (p. 51), copyright © 1978.

Gracious God, we pray for your holy catholic church: *Lutheran Book of Worship* (p. 45), copyright © 1978.

NOVEMBER

O God, our help in ages past: Text, public domain.

Psalm 34:1-8, 15-22: *Psalter for the Christian People,* copyright © 1993 The Liturgical Press. Reprinted by permission.

Almighty God, whose people are knit together in one holy church: *Lutheran Book of Worship* (p. 36), copyright © 1978.

We give thanks to you, O Lord our God: *Lutheran Book of Worship* (p. 46), copyright © 1978.

With reverence and affection we remember before you, O everlasting God: *Lutheran Book of Worship* (p. 51), copyright © 1978.

Almighty God, by the death and burial of Jesus: *Lutheran Book of Worship: Occasional Services* (p. 125), copyright © 1982.

O Lord, support us all the day long of this troubled life: *Lutheran Book of Worship* (p. 158), copyright © 1978.

Almighty God, your generous goodness comes to us new every day: *Lutheran Book of Worship* (p. 40), copyright © 1978.

Psalm 121: *Psalter for the Christian People,* copyright © 1993 The Liturgical Press. Reprinted by permission.

O God, comfort with the grace of your Holy Spirit: *Lutheran Book of Worship* (p. 53), copyright © 1978.

O God, we remember with thanksgiving: *Lutheran Book of Worship* (p. 53), copyright © 1978.

Lord Jesus, by your death you took away the sting of death: *Lutheran Book of Worship* (p. 213), copyright © 1978.